YOU CAN
SUCCEED

THE ULTIMATE STUDY GUIDE FOR STUDENTS

by Eric Jensen

Illustrations by
Charles McPherson

BARRON'S EDUCATIONAL SERIES, INC.
Woodbury, New York

"There are no limitations to the self. There are no limitations to its potential. You can adopt artificial limitations through ignorance."

Jane Roberts

All inquiries should be addressed to:
Barron's Educational Series, Inc.
113 Crossways Park Drive
Woodbury, New York 11797

Library of Congress Catalog Card No. 79-13489

International Standard Book No. 0-8120-2084-7

Library of Congress Cataloging in Publication Data
Jensen, Eric.
  You can succeed, you can become a better student.
  Bibliography: p.
  1. Study, Method of. 2. Report writing.
  3. Research. 4. Note-taking. I. Title.
LB2395.J43 371.3'02812 79-13489
ISBN 0-8120-2084-7

PRINTED IN THE UNITED STATES OF AMERICA

CONTENTS

FIGURES

TABLES

PREFACE

This book had its beginnings several years ago. I realized that there are many study guides available to students, but none have become a classic. I believe previous "how to study" books presented information but did not give the tools and motivation necessary to implement the information.

This book is different. It will provide you with much more than just information. This book will provide you with simple, effective, and dynamic tools to become a superior student. It will motivate you to use those tools each and every day, as you must do to succeed.

I began this book by compiling data from years of teaching in a highly progressive private school. I used the techniques included in this book with over 3,000 students. I inspired them to dramatic heights in the achievement of learning skills. In addition, I have researched countless books in order to simplify the path to becoming a successful student.

This book is based on my research and experience. It conveys the enthusiasm and attitude which has been proven successful time and again. This book has everything you need to become a successful student. I have enjoyed writing it and I know you will enjoy reading it. Because you chose to read this book, I know you are ready for the success you deserve. Congratulations and happy reading!

ACKNOWLEDGMENTS

With the assault of the information explosion, it becomes more and more difficult to stay current in one's field. It becomes a necessity to utilize the background, research, and support of others in writing a book. Although it would be nice to be able to say I created an entirely original book, the truth is that many were involved.

My first thoughts turn to those generous and steadfast associates and friends who gave me the encouragement and support I needed. I am grateful to: Robert Armstrong; Dr. James and Edna Ehleringer; Megan Fraenkel; Mark Huffman; John Koon; Michael and Zaida McDonald; Susie McDowell; Lee, Lisa, Peg and Dr. Norm Pliscou; Dr. Paul Saltman; John Sargent; and Kasey Thornton. I owe a special debt of gratitude to my loving and magnificent father, Dr. Robert Jensen. He has always been an inspiration and model for me.

I am especially beholden to those who helped with specific ideas, guidance, or gave me the feedback from the manuscript I needed so much. I appreciate as special: Bill and Carol Baras, Patricia Franklin, Hans and Gail Heinzerling, and Michael McDonald.

My final words of appreciation are to the three who were undeniably instrumental in this success: my typist, Kathie Schmit, my copy editor Janet Plate, and of course, Barron's Educational Series, Inc., the progressive publisher who had the courage and wisdom to produce a book needed so badly.

INTRODUCTION

Everybody likes to be successful. Yet, success is not getting A's in school, being popular, getting a scholarship, or making money. Success is a gut-level feeling of confidence and achievement. It is a powerful state of mind wherein the world is yours for the asking. It is a joyous world of unlimited opportunity and choices.

The unhappiest person is the person without choices. To acquire more choices, you need assets. The personal assets you have increase your opportunities and choices in life. Education can be a definite asset, whether formal or informal. It can open up many doors that were previously closed, so get the best education you can. Even if you don't use the academic information, you may use the contacts you make in school later on in life.

This means that you should go to the best school you can afford. It may help you get a better education and have an opportunity to associate with more successful students and staff. In addition, your school's reputation will carry with you for years.

Once you have chosen your place of education, do the very best you can. Success is an important habit to establish because good habits formed in school will be with you all your life. The whole purpose of this book is to help give you the tools to form those success habits. I applaud your decision to read and use this book. A better tool could not have been chosen!

Daily Scroll

Today, this new day, I am a successful student. Overnight my mind and body have produced thousands of new cells to give me the greatest advantages possible. I am born anew, revitalized and full of energy.

I am rare and valuable; unique in all the universe. I am nature's greatest miracle in action. I have unlimited potential. I believe in my abilities, attitudes, and goals. I am worthy of greatness because I am the most important person in my world.

Today I push myself to my limits. I use the skills and knowledge from this book every day. I begin the day with a success and end it with a success. My goals are being reached every day and I seek them eagerly.

I act positively and happily, fully accepting myself and others. I live to the fullest by experiencing life without limits. I embrace life. I approach each class, each book, and each assignment with enthusiasm, happiness, and joy. I thirst for knowledge. I look forward to reading and believing this scroll each and every day.

I am a positive and successful student. I know each step I must take to continue to be that way. I am clear on my goals and see myself reaching them. I now realize my infinite potential, thus, my burden lightens. I smile and laugh. I have become the greatest student in the world.

Figure 1.
Sample Self-Improvement Contract

———————————————
Date

Self: _____

Other: _____

AGREEMENT

Self: *I will read or study at least one hour per day. I will use my hand as a pacer, go quickly as I can and read my Daily Scroll each day, also.*

Other: *I will encourage Willie to follow his plans and be cheerful, positive, and supportive of his quest for fulfilling his goal.*

CONSEQUENCES

Arranged by Self (if contract is honored): *I will go to my favorite recreational area with my girlfriend.*

(if contract is broken): *I will do extra house and yard work for someone else for one week.*

Arranged by Other (if contract is kept): *I agree to take Willie out for dinner of his choice, and buy him two record albums.*

Signed_____
Self

———————————————
Other

CHAPTER ONE

LACK OF MOTIVATION: THE #1 PROBLEM

"There is no such thing as a problem without a gift. We seek problems because we need their gifts."

Richard Bach

Over and over again the most common problem mentioned by students is lack of motivation. "I can't seem to get motivated," is a common excuse for almost any school related problem. This chapter explores the reasons for lack of motivation and failure. Then it is followed with twelve ways to motivate yourself to excellence. Once you have understood and completed this chapter, you have taken the first and biggest step toward becoming the success you were meant to be. Read it, and see what reasons have kept you from being a total success.

ELEVEN REASONS FOR FAILURE IN SCHOOL

1. Lack of a Definite Goal.

Why are you in school? Is it to become a doctor, lawyer, or engineer? Is it to increase your awareness of current events, real estate, or human nature? Whatever the reason you go to school, you still need a specific goal to strive for. If someone asked you to get into your car and start driving, you'd first say "where to?" There's not much point in getting into your car unless you've got a goal in mind. Your goal may be to go to the store, library, or beach, but you need to know *where* before you start your engine. Students who lack a definite goal will find their incentive for excellence is weak, and their paths will often stray from the road to success.

2. Laziness.

Often a product of many other factors, laziness is a habit which can cut short even the most promising career. Laziness often stems from negative surroundings such as critical friends or relatives, and a lack of definite goals. Laziness, the opposite of decision and action, is the enemy every successful person must conquer. Successful students use their capacity to reach prompt and definite decisions, and are slow to change their minds. The failures ponder simple decisions endlessly and even then, change their mind often. Laziness is really the unwillingness to make a decision and the commitment to follow through with it.

For until you have made a strong decision on exactly what your goals are, and committed yourself to achieving them, you can expect failure. Many students have made a strong decision on what they want. But the commitment to those goals is as important as establishing them. It's not enough to say "I want an A in that class." You'll need to say, "I want an A in that class and will get one. I will study ten hours a week if that's what it takes." Therefore, your first decision must be to conquer laziness.

3. Poor Relationships.

Analyze your current relationships with loved ones, family, and friends. Are they positive, encouraging, productive, and helpful? Or are they negative, discouraging, and counter-productive? If you constantly fight with or worry about your mate, you're using up valuable time and energy. How about your mother or father? Are they putting unnecessary pressure upon you to perform in school? You don't need that. Either set them straight that it is *your* life and *your* choices, or learn to cope better with their parenting role. How about your friends? Are they a joy to be with, positive about their lives, and undemanding of your time? If they are not, you need to make some changes. Poor relationships can ruin even the best student.

4. Poor Study Habits.

Each year over one million students drop out of school. In college, only one of three freshmen will graduate. One of the reasons most often mentioned is "I can't keep up." Don't fall into the same trap. If your study skills are weak, improve them! There are many ways that you can go about it! Don't write off a career because you can't read or study well. The sad truth is that few schools teach study skills effectively. Some of the most valuable skills such as speed reading, concentration, comprehension, memorizing, note-taking, and analysis are neglected. But they are available from private sources such as tutoring and study groups, and of course, in this book. Learn them, and more importantly, *use* them.

5. Excessive Worry.

Many students waste hours and even days fretting and worrying over their school work or personal life. This expends energy that is necessary for other areas. The proper feeling should be concern: a normal, healthy, and necessary caring for what you do. When you worry excessively you can become paralyzed by an upcoming event or obsessed by a current problem. If you can do something about a problem, go do it. If you can't forget it easily, use the method described in the next chapter. It works!

6. Negative Personality Traits.

Of all the years of one's life, those of greatest change are from ages eighteen to twenty-five, the "student" years. As rapid emotional, physical, and social growth takes place, we must make adjustments in our self-image and life style. Those who are unable or unwilling to make the adjustments, unable to "flow with"

A NEGATIVE PERSONALITY
WILL SURELY BRING FAILURE...

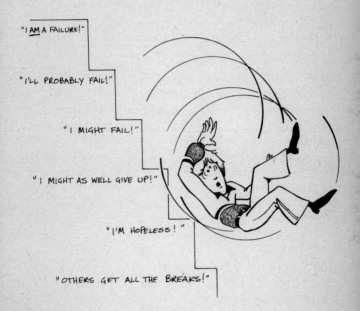

"I AM A FAILURE!"

"I'LL PROBABLY FAIL!"

"I MIGHT FAIL!"

"I MIGHT AS WELL GIVE UP!"

"I'M HOPELESS!"

"OTHERS GET ALL THE BREAKS!"

the changes, may express their frustrations through other outlets. Some of these outlets may be shyness, sarcasm, criticism, withdrawal, guilt, listlessness, or using alibis. All of these negative personality traits can make good study habits difficult or impossible. Excessive shyness and withdrawn behavior may lead to criticism by others or unhealthy emotional growth. Sarcasm, though often used in fun, is a destructive and extremely negative habit. What's worse is that a sarcastic individual is often unaware of the impact of his sharp comments. Guilt and criticism often go together. Highly critical individuals often vent their guilt feelings through criticism of others, directing the blame they think they deserve upon others. There are, of course, countless alibis that poor students use. Alibis are tools of those who do not wish to accept responsibility for their own lives. Alibis will always give a poor achiever justification for mediocrity. A student with negative personality traits almost invites failure.

7. Outside Activities.

Everyone has only twenty-four hours in a day, seven days in a week. Those who try to cram twenty-five hours into a twenty-four hour day often become ineffective. Thomas Edison, when asked to explain his success, said it was the result of concentrating on only one thing at a time. Most people try to do so many things at once that their scattered efforts cannot possibly be as potent as if all of their efforts were focused on one activity. The most common outside activities which inhibit student progress are belonging to too many clubs, watching too much television, and spending too much time with friends or excessive hours at work. Proper budgeting of time is essential for success.

8. Lack of Incentive or Interest.

If you lack a good reason to do well, you need to develop desire. A dull, listless student who lacks interest in school will certainly not have the motivation to efficiently study. Most poor students have not become sufficiently interested in the subject to develop the necessary energy to do well. It is an absolute necessity to care about what you study. Lack of caring often stems from negative personality traits, poor relationships, or lack of an exact goal in school.

9. Illness.

Doctors and behaviorists estimate an incredible seventy to ninety-five percent of all illnesses are unintentionally self-induced. The medical term *psychosomatic* includes an endless assortment of illnesses which include stomach aches, migraine headaches, fevers, and allergies. If you are consistently plagued by any of these illnesses, you need to look at why it happens. If you get a stomach ache before studying, are you trying to avoid studying? If your health is not good, look for some reasons why. The reasons may not be purely physical. As a child, we learned that being sick allowed us to stay home from school, miss assignments, and get pampered by our parents. There were certainly rewards for being sick, and some of those rewards still exist. You may be doing something similar now, whether consciously or subconsciously. Check your environment to see if there are any payoffs or benefits for your sickness. If so, you may be able to discover the true source of your illness and cure it. Persistent illness can cause missed classes and assignments, encouraging failure.

10. Lack of Intellectual Ability.

Lack of intelligence is the least likely of all reasons for student failure. Anyone who chooses to read this book probably does not have a lack of ability. A battery of aptitude or IQ tests will give you the answer if you're in doubt.

11. Other Reasons.

You can fill in any reason not previously mentioned that you feel is a impediment to success. But whatever problems you list, realize that ninety-nine percent of them can be solved. Failure always has its alibi, but success requires no explanation.

TWELVE STEPS TO ACHIEVING SELF-MOTIVATION

1. Set a Goal.

It is essential that you establish clearly defined goals for yourself. Students who already have a specific goal in mind such as a career in writing, medicine, acting, law or engineering may need to make their goals more specific. It is not enough to say "I want to be a scientist." You should decide what field you wish to study and when you plan to enter that field. The time commitment you set up is important. By setting a date for goal completion, you have created a pressure to perform. This self-induced motivation will help you towards your goal by encouraging better decision-making. Instead of being confused and paralyzed by many alternatives, your time commitment will narrow your choices by its limitations. Then you can quickly choose the alternative which takes you toward your goal. Setting personal goals and achieving them can be tremendously satisfying.

Students need to set both long and short range goals for themselves. Short range goals may be those which can be accomplished in two to ten weeks. Such goals must be specific: "I want to get straight A's this term." Longer range goals may be to graduate with highest honors, to get a scholarship, to be accepted to a higher institute of learning, or to pursue a particular field. Your goals, of course, may include more personal objectives such as wanting to become more positive, generous, or even to earn a certain amount of money. Remember ninety-eight of one hundred students who are classified as failures had no goal, or specific aim. If you do not know what you want as a goal, find one through experience. Attend lectures, travel, take unusual classes, and meet varied and interesting people. Most students without goals simply have not had enough life experiences to have found what they like. Once you do find what you like, announce your goal to your friends and family. By announcing your goal you'll reinforce its meaning to yourself and, you will allow others to encourage and support you. Always broadcast your goals, never your accomplishments or successes. Others will gladly support and applaud your fulfilled dreams. It is finding and setting a goal which is critical. Whatever the goal, set a long or short range one immediately, so you can begin enjoying the benefits.

Use a self-improvement contract, instead of just talking about goals, set them right now. Decide upon a definite, specific goal for this term in school. What would you like to accomplish? To make the honor roll? To excel in an outside school activity? Become clear on your goal, and write it down on a self-improvement contract like the sample shown in Figure 1. Have a close friend or relative co-sign the contract. Compare your contract to the sample contract to be sure yours is done properly.

First, date it and fill in your name and the "other" person's name. Write the specific goal you wish to accomplish. Then write your agreement. The agreement is how you plan to achieve your goal. What will you do each day or each week that will advance yourself towards your goal? The consequences are rewards if you honor your contract. There are also punishments if you fail to honor it. You should work these out with the person with whom you sign the contract. Make sure you both have something to lose and something to gain. Once you've completed your contract and signed it, post it in your house as a reminder of the obligation you have to yourself and the co-signer. The following questions can provide ideas for rewards:

1. What kinds of things do you like to have?
2. What are your major interests?
3. What fun hobbies do you enjoy most?
4. Who do you like to spend time with?
5. What do you like to do with those people?
6. What do you do for fun?
7. How do you get away from it all?
8. What ways do you like to relax?
9. What makes you feel proud or happy?
10. What would be a nice gift to receive?
11. If you just found $5, how would you spend it? How about $10, or even $50?

Now some suggestions.

Going horseback riding
Eating a favorite fruit or dessert
Reading a great book
Playing golf, volleyball, bridge, or jogging
Camping or escaping for the weekend
Taking a day off work
Enjoying your favorite meal
Buying yourself or loved one a gift
Watching your favorite TV show
Going for a walk in the park or along the beach
Playing with some kids

Going to beauty salon
Seeing your favorite movie
Eating a midnite snack
Eating at your favorite restaurant
Hiring someone for a day - a gardener or
    maid
Doing something creative; writing,
    building, painting or taking photos
Taking a short nap
Getting a suntan
Going on an unusual trip
Doing absolutely nothing
Cooking or baking
Working in the garden
Skateboarding, skiing, or skating
Visiting friends or relatives
Going shopping

2. Build Desire.

Once your goals are formulated, you need to light the fire and begin to fan it. There are several good ways to build a strong, desire to fulfill goals. First of all, visualize your goals strongly and clearly every day. Take a minute out of your busy schedule to relax. Close your eyes and picture yourself strongly, vividly, and clearly reaching your goal. Practice this visualization every day, and the desire will build. Desire, like setting a goal, is only the starting point. It is essential to build the desire through affirmation of your specific goal, a definite plan, and then fuel the dreams with the power of your constant and creative imagination. Remember there is no hope for those students who lack the basic desire to excel. They are unlikely to succeed.

3. Think Rationally.

Learn to use your mind constructively and to your advantage all the time. Don't allow yourself to become paralyzed by irrational or unnecessary thoughts. Have an open, receptive, and clear mind which is free from dogma, superstition, and prejudice. Find out about those things you are not sure of! Do not substitute guesses for thinking. Many students get poor grades because they made incorrect assumptions throughout a course. Don't guess or assume the professor will want something. Ask! Use the power of rational thinking to motivate yourself to new heights. If you're having trouble motivating yourself to do homework, ask yourself if it would be to your benefit to get an *A* in that class. If it would, decide whether you are willing to pay the price. Strike a bargain with yourself. It makes sense to get the best grade you can for the energy you're willing to spend. The skills you are learning from this book will enable you to get top grades at a better "price" (in terms of your own effort).

Once you have established your goals and accepted that you desire them, then the motivation to do homework is necessary. So instead of rationalizing excuses *not* to do something, you can use rational thinking as a reason *to* do something. The power of your rational mind is sufficient to overcome most of your failure-prone habits. Simply stop, and re-evaluate your old beliefs. The following lists will help you see the advantages of good study habits and the disadvantages of not developing good study habits:

*Consider the benefits of successful study habits:

Studying takes less time

Self-image improves

Gain better comprehension

Less frustration and re-reading

Sharpen thinking habits

Better grades

Chances for scholarships

Better qualified for career opportunities

Gain more knowledge

Greater confidence in academic and social areas

Explore personal potential.

*Consider the costs of *not* changing study habits:

Studying will be time-consuming

Poor self-image

Unnecessary poor comprehension

Discouraging and frustrating study sessions

Unclear thinking

Poor grades

Less qualified for jobs

Know less material

Lack of self-confidence

Unfulfilled personal potential

Lower chances for getting scholarships

Rational Thinking Builds Success Habits...

*Consider the "benefits" of poor study habits:

Avoid responsibilities and demands from others which require reading skills

Less pressure from others-no risk or failure

Don't threaten others by "outshining" them

Sympathy and attention gained from others who feel sorry for your failures in school

13

What is your *rational* decision on study habits?

Suppose that you wish to re-examine your belief that other students get all the breaks and that you'll never graduate with honors. In *Psycho-Cybernetics,* Dr. Maxwell Maltz suggests you ask yourself four important questions:

1. "Is there any rational reason for such a belief?
2. Could it be that I am mistaken in this belief?
3. Would I come to the same conclusion about some other person in a similar situation?
4. Why should I continue to act and feel as if this were true if there is no good reason to believe it?"

Now, scrutinize your belief through these questions and think it out carefully. Most of the time you'll find that your belief holds no factual basis and that it disappears. The power of rational thinking is a powerful tool to use in improving yourself. Don't ignore it. The mind has no limitations except those which you acknowledge.

4. Develop Positive Personality Traits.

Positive personality traits include, both attitudes and opinions. A positive person attracts other positive people, thus enabling mutual support and inspiration. A student with a positive outlook is enthusiastic about life, has a healthy self-image, and makes decisions promptly. This same student is also honest, dependable, and tolerant. A positive personality makes you enjoyable to be with. Start with your attitude. That's simply your

A POSITIVE PERSONALITY
BRINGS SURE SUCCESS...

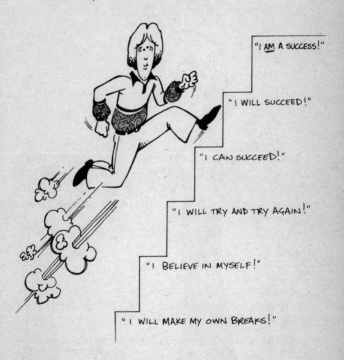

CHOOSE FRIENDS CAREFULLY!

relationship with yourself. Do you get along well by yourself, trust yourself, and believe in yourself? If you do believe in yourself, you know you can and will succeed in school. This positive attitude will allow you to handle difficult assignments, demanding teachers, and social pressures. When you are confident and positive, others know they can depend on you. Therefore, they develop confidence in you and can help you reach your goals faster.

If you do not believe in yourself, it is important to change that programming. Read the Daily Scroll and you'll certainly want to utilize The Secret at the end of the book. And a positive personality goes well with a healthy mind and body. Eat lightly. Eat the proper balance of health-giving, wholesome foods. Exercise regularly and learn proper posture. Take care of your hair, teeth, nails, and complexion. Hold your head high and smile. Read as much as you can, informing yourself in fields like philosophy and psychology. Reduce your egotism and replace it with a balance of healthy confidence and modesty. A positive personality is a must for putting into action your desires, plans, and goals.

5. Choose Friends Carefully.

Many students never stop to think about some of the strongest influences on their lives. The people you see the most often affect you the greatest. Most people tend to have a general life style that is similar to their friends. An important implication is that you'd better choose your friends carefully because in doing so, you choose your future. By associating with those who are your model, you are most apt to make some pleasant changes in yourself.

So if your friends are talented, considerate of others, healthy, happy and well-rounded, then you are likely to acquire those traits also. Or, if your friends are high achievers who enter science or hobby fairs, become involved in athletics, drama, singing, or good jobs, you'll feel those influences, too.

Yet, the opposite is also true. The saying "Birds of a feather flock together," has been proven accurate. You may acquire some poor habits if your friends are unsupportive, act tough, abuse drugs, drifting without goals, or are in legal trouble. These so-called friends can set you back years by leading you away from your own goals.

Friends with positive personalities are strongest in the categories of friendliness, honesty, and communication skills. Friendliness is important because everyone needs good quality friends, and only by being a positive, happy person will you attract good friends. Honesty is the corner-stone of a good personality because it is the advertisement of your values. By being honest, you'll avoid embarrassing problems such as having to cover one lie with another. Or, worse yet, being confronted with the truth later on. Communication is an essential part of a positive personality because most people do not read minds, and verbal messages are the best we can do. Be direct, honest, and square with your thoughts and feelings. It will save many headaches later on and help you earn the healthy respect of others.

16

If a friend is not a positive experience for you and much of the time you have disagreements, you need to make some changes. Either spend less time with that friend, or figure out how to get along better. It's important to have a confidant or study partner, and maybe one person is both. But if you have a specific goal to reach, and if this "friend" is constantly pouring out their problems to you and infringing upon your peace of mind or time, wake up! You don't have to stay in any relationship, regardless of whether or not they "need" you. Regardless of their needs, they do not have the right to ruin your happiness or your chance of reaching your goal. A good school mate can be a dynamic source of inspiration, knowledge, and enjoyment. By choosing positive, growing friends you will find the path much easier. But most agree, it is necessary to choose your friends carefully.

6. Have Faith in Yourself.

The starting point for success in school, even before goals and desire, is trust. If you don't believe in yourself, there's no point in trying, is there? Self-trust and faith are essential. "If you think you're beaten, you are," means those without faith in themselves will surely fail. Faith is the basis of all miracles and the basis for all success. You must believe in this essential fact: What the mind can conceive and believe, it can achieve. People have used their faith and mind to stop their own heartbeat, walk on hot coals, and stop from bleeding. So it can certainly be used more effectively to get *A's*.

17

Maybe you've been thinking that you need that "something extra" to succeed. Do you think you lack tools, resources, opportunity, creativity, or intelligence? Forget that negative thinking. You have not been short-changed! Let's take inventory to find out what you really have going for you.

Your marvelous eyes have a hundred million sensory receptors with which to enjoy the world. You can watch a sunset, read a book, or see a loved one. Count one asset!

And through the courtesy of a complex, well-engineered hearing system you can listen beautifully. You can hear a concert, a waterfall, or a friendly voice. Count another asset!

Your trained voice can speak any language in the world. You can laugh, whisper, or shout for joy. Count another asset!

Your incredible body has over 500 muscles, 200 bones, and 60 miles of veins and arteries to serve you. Yet it tirelessly builds thousands of new cells daily and features a heart which beats over 100,000 times and pumps over 1,600 gallons a day without complaint. Count yet another asset!

Do you complain of a lack of wealth? Your personal wealth is endless! What rich man, old and feeble would not gladly exchange all money, property, gold, stocks, and bonds for the blessings you have taken for granted? To create a computer nearly equal to your brain, it would cost over ten billion dollars. Don't treat yourself lightly! It would take up as much space as the Empire State Building and require the water of the Mississippi River just to cool it. You master-mind a ten billion dollar super computer which features memory banks, creativity, and logic components. It controls millions of pain, touch, and temperature detectors all over your body which can help you adjust to burning deserts, the sea, polar ice caps, outer space, and even classes at school.

You are the greatest creation the world has ever seen. You are the technological pinnacle of mankind. Your list of personal assets is endless and you must acknowledge those treasures to become successful. Never again complain that you need "something extra." You are one-of-a-kind and unique among the seventy billion humans who have ever lived. Enjoy the rarity you have. Use your assets to become the student you know you can be.

You can develop faith in yourself several ways. The best two ways include accepting yourself as you are and as the person you can become. The preceding paragraphs and your Daily Scroll will help you if you read them often. If you ever lacked faith about your potential as a student, the fears will diminish. The mind will accept as truth anything, if it is repeated and reinforced enough.

The second way to develop confidence and faith in yourself is through actions. Set up short, easily attainable goals for yourself and watch your successes pile up. Then focus your memory and present thoughts on your virtues. This gives a stronger picture of yourself, thus building faith also.

7. Give Reinforcement.

The best way to get more of what you want is to reward the source when the desired behavior is produced. This is known as positive reinforcement. Set up a reward system for yourself for long and short term goals. When you accomplish a short term goal such as getting an *A* on a mid-term, then reward yourself with something you value. You may want to give yourself a dinner, concert, day at the beach, an item of clothing, or a record. Be fair to yourself and only reward yourself when you achieve your goal. Rewards are the whole principle behind the self-improvement contract introduced earlier in this chapter. Reward the positive and, if appropriate, punish the negative.

One mistake many people make when trying to use a reward system is delaying the rewards or offering them at intervals too great to be effective. Set up a reward system which can be administered at short intervals. Never more than a week should pass without at least some temporary rewards. When used properly, a program of positive reinforcement can bring about the desired habits with ease.

8. Get Specialized Knowledge.

Since your goal is to become an exceptional student, learn the techniques used by the experts. Take this book seriously, and use it thoroughly. Seek counseling or tutoring if necessary. Having poor study skills is one of the major causes of student failure, but an easy one to remedy.

9. Consider the Use of Autosuggestion.

Also known as self-hypnosis, autosuggestion enables much of the changing process within you to happen automatically. Although everyone has control over their minds, most do not exercise that control to the maximum. This explains why the schools are full of failing and disappointed students. The steps to effective use of your mind through auto or self-suggestion are simple. First of all, get in a relaxed position and positive state of mind. State your exact goal, the date you plan to achieve it, and the method you'll use. Say this out loud, and pronounce the words with feeling and emotion. Your mind will not act on commands without the necessary spirit within them. Then, visualize yourself clearly, having accomplished your goal, and hold that mental picture for a minute while your mind learns to accept its new role. Repeat these steps each and every day. Do not be discouraged if it seems crazy at first. Autosuggestion through these visualization techniques generally takes at least twenty-one days or more to be most effective, but the results are rewarding. The final chapter in this book will go into self-hypnosis in greater detail.

Another very effective form of autosuggestion is using "mentalization" techniques. Provided in the front of this book is a Daily Scroll. By reading and believing the scroll each and every day, your mind will become so saturated with the ideals of success that it will act upon the words without effort. Soon you'll have the scroll memorized, and its benefits, its uplifting and motivating power, will continue daily with each reading. Post the scroll in a place where you can see it every day. It will soon become a favorite part of your day.

10. Solve Personal Problems.

If personal situations are on your mind, it is difficult to concentrate, no matter how good your study skills are. Car problems, poor health, or romantic involvements are a part of life, but there is no reason why these should dominate. The student years are often the most traumatic portion of one's life. It seems that everything that could happen, does. But outside events don't have to be catastrophes if you keep them in perspective. Most are really not the disasters they are made out to be.

One mistake consistently made in dealing with personal problems is avoiding them because of "overthinking." This means making assumptions about what we perceive will or will not happen. These assumptions often immobilize an otherwise clear-thinking individual. Don't assume there is a problem, but confront the person involved. Try to clear it up early. Be direct, honest, and warm. Communicate your feelings first, then your thoughts. Listen to the other side before deciding upon a course of action. But take the situation into your hands and deal with it. Avoiding it only postpones it and amplifies the problem. Make an effort to not "overthink" or avoid personal problems, and they will become less worry for you.

Most personal conflicts go away in time, but it's rarely worth it to wait that long. Almost every school has a qualified counseling staff that can help you to solve difficult problems. Chances are good that they have already dealt with and solved problems very similar to yours.

11. Develop Persistence.

Consider the following proverb:

> Nothing in the world can take the place of persistence.
>
> Talent will not, nothing is more common than unsuccessful men with talent.
>
> Genius will not, unrewarded genius is almost a proverb.
>
> Education will not, the world is full of educated derelicts.
>
> Persistence and determination alone are omnipotent.

While motivation is essential to begin the path to success, only persistence will keep you on the path. Motivation is like fuel for your car; it gets you going toward your goal. But cars will run out of gas unless the persistence is there to refuel. The starting point for developing persistence is to have something to persist toward. Have an exact and desirable goal in mind and keep it there. Your motivation will move you to action, but your persistence will keep you moving. Persistence is insured, provided these six qualities are developed.

Desire. Essential to success is the intense desire for achievement. A strong desire indicates your willingness to persist in making sacrifices to reach your goal. Your strong desire will help put you in the right place at the right time. Finally, your strong desire will keep the bonfires of persistence burning.

Self-reliance. Confidence in yourself will allow you to be persistent. You must have exceptional faith in your own abilities because you will be tried and tested many times on your path to success. You must learn to rely on yourself because there is no one else to rely on. You may fail dozens of times, but your next effort may bring a success. You'll never know how close success is until you take that one extra step. You were not born a failure nor will you become one. One step at a time, and only one step at a time is necessary. You may liken yourself to an acorn which becomes a mighty tree and eventually builds a forest. Countless success stories arose from failures who refused to give up. Your confidence will help strengthen the persistence you need.

Reinforcement. There are three excellent ways to reinforce your persistence. Keep exact goals posted conspicuously where you live, work, and drive. You should see reminders of your goals everywhere you go. If your goal is to get into Harvard Law School, get a picture of it and put that picture up in your bathroom, on your refrigerator door, or on the dash board of your car. This reinforcement will help your subconscious mind work towards that goal. It will help remind you of the goal you are striving for.

A second way to reinforce your persistence is through successes. Set temporary, short, easily attainable goals and meet them. The more successes you gain, the greater the personal ego reinforcement. It's difficult to lack confidence when you are being successful each and every day.

You can receive reinforcement from positive friends. Encouraging, supportive, and enthusiastic friends can help inspire and push you along the path to success. So be sure to choose your friends carefully, as they can and will influence your success patterns.

Mastery of Habits. Self-control is another essential step toward persistence. You must become the true master of your own personal habits. Negative habits such as over-indulgence, poor health, criticizing others, financial mismanagement, or poor use of time can be lessened and maintained at less destructive levels. To help self-control, post positive reminders such as notecards in your house with your new habits written down. By constant reminder and desire, you'll be able to control those poor habits.

Courage. Every successful person must have the personal courage and conviction of faith to maintain persistence. You must ignore criticism from others and keep your own plans and goals in mind. It will take courage to maintain a positive nature while others fire the arrows of negativism and criticism. But read the scroll each day, and it will affirm your goals and beliefs giving the courage you need to act positively.

Positive Mental Attitude. A crucial step toward maintaining persistence is to have strong personal optimism. Keep your mind tightly closed against negative people and thoughts. Eliminate negative words from your vocabulary such as impossible, can't, won't, defeat, failure, or unworkable. Do not allow yourself to think about the negative side of things. A positive mental attitude means you are confident of your own ability to succeed, and you refuse to associate with those who think otherwise.

Think, believe, and act in a positive manner. There is no substitute for a continuous effort. The schools are full of students who make half-hearted efforts, and who end up with poor grades and an incomplete, inadequate education. The most common reasons for lack of persistence are lack of intense desire for a specific goal and lack of faith in yourself. Many people are too easily discouraged by failures. Many begin to see themselves as failures simply because they were not successful at some specific task. But *you* are not a failure, no matter how many times you do not live up to your expectations. Thomas Edison said he had nearly 10,000 failures on the path to producing the electric light bulb. Did he give up? Of course not, and he said he didn't mind failure at all because he learned from every one. Each failure taught him how *not* to do it the next time. In school, learn from your tests. When you get a low grade, find out why, so you can prepare better for the next test. Continuous, applied effort, without giving up, is a sure way to become successful. Successful students lead the parade of fulfillment, achievement, and happiness while the unsuccessful sit on the sidelines. Most students show sporadic promise in school, but the achievers have made the consistent effort through their will power. The achievers begin with strong desire for an exact purpose, continue with faith in themselves, and then follow through with the habit of using willpower.

26

A success will not give up. He or she will explore and exhaust all possibilities and alternatives. Many problems go unsolved because someone gave up and lost the desire to continue. A genius does not wait for a magical bolt of inspiration. It takes hard work and long hours to produce. Edison rightly said, "Genius is ten percent inspiration and ninety percent perspiration." And he should know. He holds more U.S. patents than any other man. Yet, he experienced thousands of failures in his career. So be willing to invest your time and energy - ideas don't work unless you do.

12. Take Action.

Every desire, every plan, every bit of knowledge is useless unless followed by action. No battle plan has ever won a war, no law ever prevented a crime, no book ever read itself. Action is the key. Repeat it to yourself over and over again. Action is the key. Do not wait for tomorrow. Tomorrow may never come. Do not wait for the time to be right. The time is right now. Do not worry about what to do, or how to do it. Just say when. Say now. Begin this moment. This precious moment which will never come again. This priceless day, which will end in just a few hours, must be utilized. Live each day to the fullest through action. Would you be proud to say how you spent today, maybe the last of your life? Put your alibis and excuses away. Open up your eyes, your heart, your mind. Embrace life, laugh, and have fun. But most of all, act, and act now. Action is the only thing which will reap the rewards you want. It's the single most potent ingredient to success. Do not delay. You have but one life, and you must not waste today, possibly the last and most precious day of your life. Make today the culmination of your desires, plans, and knowledge. Act now and become a successful student.

REVIEW THESE POINTS

*Eleven Reasons for Failure
1. Lack of a Definite Goal
2. Laziness
3. Poor Relationships
4. Poor Study Habits
5. Excessive Worry
6. Negative Personality Traits
7. Outside Activities
8. Lack of Incentive or Interest
9. Illness
10. Lack of Intellectual Ability
11. Other Reasons

*Twelve Steps to Achieving Self-Motivation
1. Set a goal.
2. Build Desire.
3. Think Rationally.
4. Develop Positive Personality Traits.
5. Choose Friends Carefully.
6. Have Faith in Yourself.
7. Give Reinforcement.
8. Get Specialized Knowledge.
9. Consider the Use of Autosuggestion.
10. Solve Personal Problems.
11. Develop Persistence.
12. Take Action.

Figure 2.
A Guide for Preparing to Read

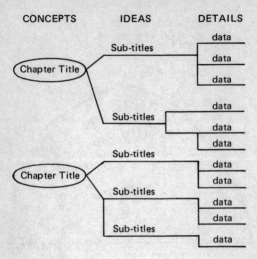

CHAPTER TWO

SUCCESS HABITS: BEGIN NOW

"In brief, sir, study what you most affect."
Shakespeare

SUCCESSFUL SCHOOL HABITS

In 1912 Harry Wilson wrote an interesting story named *"Bunker Bean"*. It's the saga of a man who was tricked into believing in himself. Bunker was a man who was penniless and orphaned as a child. As an adult, he lived in a cheap boarding house suffering a life of frustration and poverty. But a false spiritualistic medium moved into his boarding house and convinced him to give up part of his wages in exchange for psychic readings. The psychic told Bunker that life progressed in vast karmic cycles and that although Bunker's life was very negative, he was completing the lower half of a cycle. The upcoming portion of his life was to be the exact opposite and he was to take on the successful qualities of Napoleon. Bunker believed the psychic and began assuming the virtues of his new role model. After reading and following books on Napoleon, Bunker became such a success that his friends and employer could hardly believe the changes. Over a period of time the new success habits became such a part of him that even when he found out the psychic was a fake, it didn't matter. His successful habits had become a permanent part of his life.

The point of the story that once successful habits are formed, they will be with you until you form new ones. In school, the successful habits you learn and use now will benefit you later in life. So, let's look at some of the important habits for school success.

Improve Your Self-image.

How do you see yourself? Do you think of yourself as a good or poor student? One of the most dramatic psychological discoveries of the twentieth century has been the uncovering of the "self-image." Whether you realize it or not, all of your actions, feelings, and behavior are consistent with your conception of yourself. The beautiful thing about that fact is it can be changed. There are thousands of students who see themselves as poor students, feel that way, hang around other poor students, and consequently become failures. Why? They "prove" themselves right by becoming the failures they thought they were.

Don't confuse self-image with positive thinking. They are not the same. Positive thinking is believing that things will turn out well whether it's plausible or not. But by improving your self-image, you are getting at

the source, the only thing you have true control over: you. So, starting today, begin picturing yourself as a good student. The purpose of a creative, mental picture is simple. First, it enables you to see the end product, and thereby become comfortable with the "new you". Whatever kind of person you would like to be or whatever changes you would like to make, the change has to come from within. By becoming comfortable with the "future" you, your subconscious can begin to direct your thoughts and actions accordingly. Your new mental picture can actually provide you with a "mental mold" or model for your actions by keeping the desired behavior in mind.

You will become what you think about, dream about, and desire to be the most. Benjamin Franklin said we should practice what we wish to become, not what we are. That's the second benefit of mental pictures. You can become the person for whom you act out the role. Often called role-playing, most of us have already done it in one form or another. Often movie actors find that by playing one role for too long, they actually do take on characteristics of that role. Playing a role can actually help you become it!

Proper mental picturing takes about two minutes a day. Sit or lie comfortably, and close your eyes. Use your imagination to create a strong, clear picture of yourself doing the desired behavior. Make the picture alive, imagining the sights and sounds of you successfully studying. Picture yourself zipping through a textbook, giving a great report in class, or getting an *A* on a test. Sound strange? Remember this: if you can't even imagine yourself getting *A's,* what hope is there for the real thing?

To become an *A* student you have got to believe it's possible for you first. Associate with other good students and acquire the study skills taught in this book. Miracles will begin as soon as you see yourself as an *A* student because you *are* one when you believe in yourself.

Rigid Schedules Are Not Necessary.

There is no relationship between a strict schedule and good grades. Just as many *A* students have strict schedules as have no schedules. Should you use a schedule? If you have a tendency to procrastinate, use one. Those who need schedules will find that they can pinpoint effective times for study. A schedule can help remind you of your school commitments and prevent careless oversights.

A weekly study schedule should be a general list of your major time commitments. Include classes, athletics, work schedules, or social engagements. Keep this weekly schedule to insure the obvious is not forgotten. Then keep a daily appointment, errand, and "to do" list of smaller commitments. At the end of the day, cross off those things you've completed, and carry the remaining tasks over to the next day. This really increases goal orientation and builds your success image through daily achievement.

Avoid Pre-study Rituals.

There are an almost unlimited number of distractions which mysteriously pop up just before studying. At times, studying seems so boring that almost anything is more interesting. Learn to avoid pre-study tactics as preparing a snack, staring at the ceiling, becoming drowsy or feeling the desire to visit friends. Your studying will become easier and easier. Most things are done out of habit, not out of need, so think about whether you really need those usual rituals. Form consistent positive study habits of getting assigned work done on time. Only then will you become the master of your school habits.

Psych Yourself Into Studying.

Pre-study blues kill more good intentions because a poor attitude can be devastating. Instead of complaining, tell yourself, "I'm going to get this material and get it fast." Decide on what you need to learn and in how much time it will take you to cover the required material. If you approach your task with a positive, receptive, open mind, you will go much faster. If you *believe* you can move through the text rapidly, half the battle is won.

Above all, don't let yourself get discouraged by thick books or imposing titles. Set up short, easily attainable goals and count your successes as you move unhesitatingly through even the toughest material. Almost any material can be broken up into a format style. Separate difficult reading into catagories, for example, introduction, examples, background, opinions, and facts. Then the material will become much more readable.

Develop Concentration.

Find the right time for study. Do it when you are most efficient and receptive to information, not when a schedule says so. Some students are "night" people, those who are just getting ready to study around midnight, while others prefer daylight. Find the proper place for studying by using the same desk each time if possible. The same desk creates familiarity and comfort which aids in getting started each time.

"If you want to be outstanding in any field, there is one important rule to observe: "Concentrate." Get one thing in your mind and heart and bloodstream. Put side blinders on your eyes so you cannot see all the distractions and temptations along the way. Forget the sidelines, and then put all the steam you've got right on the piston head and drive with full power down the main track. Keep out of the mud puddles; stay on the rails. Keep off the detours and sidings and drive straight ahead without continual startings and stoppings." Keep your mind on what you are doing. That helps create a good "mental set" for studying. Remove the usual distractions such as phone, calendar of upcoming events, television, and pin-ups. Anything you have that stimulates daydreaming will destroy your concentration. The ideal noise for study is "white noise," a term used to describe a low-level background sound which masks outside distractions. Ideally, you can use instrumental music, a bubbling aquarium, or even a steady traffic flow. These noises help equalize the extremes of dead quiet and unbearable annoyances.

Set realistic study goals. Don't tell yourself, "I'm not getting out of this chair until I know this chemistry book." Rather, set a realistic goal such as, "I'm going to learn Chapters Six and Seven within an hour." Focus energy on just one topic at a time.

It takes special concentration to eliminate the mental clutter which often impairs good study habits. Any obvious impediment to concentration should be removed. Before concentration is automatic, take care of any immediate needs such as hunger.

Use Visualization Techniques.

Sit in a relaxed position and close your eyes. Imagine a huge chalkboard in your mind. Fill the chalkboard with pictures of your concerns, problems, and worries. Get a vivid picture and hold it for a few seconds. Now, in your imagination, pick up an eraser. Beginning in the upper left hand corner of the chalkboard, slowly erase all your problems. Sometimes it requires you to "press hard" or "erase" over again in your imagination, but it always clears the problems from your head. Another effective technique involves using a piece of notepaper. These four steps are important to follow exactly:

1. Write down a description of your most pressing problem.
2. Write down at least two possible solutions to the problem. There is always more than one solution, so think hard until you come up with some alternative actions to take.
3. Write down exactly when you plan to do something about the problem. On what date

and at what time do you plan to implement your solutions?
4. Fold the piece of paper in half. While you are still looking at it, put it away in a desk or drawer.

This system has the advantage of taking the problem out of your head, removing the worry of what to do, and eliminating the decision of when to do it. Let the paper carry the burden of the problem. Once you can eliminate unnecessary or negative thoughts, your mind can focus on more urgent or scholastic matters.

Take an Interest in School.

An important attribute of good students is a strong interest in school. If you aren't interested in your classes, either you shouldn't be taking them, or you should try to generate some interest in them. Normally, interest is an automatic factor, but if it is not so with you, check over the previous chapter on motivation. Set a goal and stick to it. Students with interest in their courses invariably do better in them. Meet other students and share interests with them. In almost every subject you study, you can find some aspect that interests you. The knowledge you build from that interest leads to good grades and fosters more interest. One of the worst enemies of poor students is low morale and feelings of hopelessness. By becoming interested in your classes, classmates, and professors you will generate more morale and enthusiasm. This will help you want to do well and help you have more fun in school.

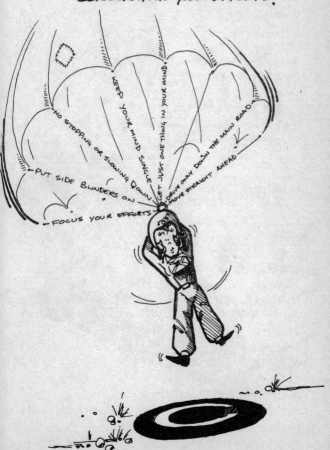

Prepare Yourself.

Start your school day by putting forth your best effort. Check over your personal appearance. Research confirms that first impressions are usually correct. So, make the first impression a good one. Wear clothes that reinforce your image as a student and learner. Conservative, academic styles often impress instructors on a subconscious, if not conscious level. In many schools, a teacher would be much more favorably impressed by a student in a dressy outfit carrying a briefcase than one in a sweatshirt, jeans, and sandals. Appropriate clothing can certainly help you feel better and enhance your self-image. Make sure you have the books, papers, and other supplies you'll need for class.

Attend Class Regularly.

There are two cases when missing class can be beneficial. The first is when you urgently need that time to prepare for an exam or write a paper, and the second is when ill health makes it inadvisable to attend. Regular attendance assures you'll have all the necessary lecture notes for exams and allows you the opportunity to clarify your understanding of any textbook reading while it's still fresh in your mind.

Be Punctual.

Get to class on time. It irritates teachers when late students interrupt their lectures. It is advisable to bring some assignment or reading to class in case the teacher is late.

Then you can still make good use of your time. Arriving early will also allow you to get the seat you want near the front of the class. Sitting in the front will help you hear more easily, see visual aids clearly, and show your teacher you're more interested in the class.

Choose an Appropriate Study Area.

It helps to study in familiar places each time because it enables you to develop a quick consistent pattern for concentration. Otherwise you may spend the first twenty minutes of your study time getting familiar with a new desk, chair, room scenery and passersby. Generally, it's not advisable to study on your bed because it's so comfortable, you may end up sleeping instead of studying. Study in an area where the lighting is indirect, yet strong; it should also be reasonably quiet. Make sure the book you are reading is fourteen to eighteen inches from your eyes. By keeping your book at this distance, eye fatigue will be lessened.

Two things you can do to help spend your study time more efficiently are setting study goals and allowing a study recess. Be sure to set short, easily attainable goals. Every hour, take a five minute break for refreshments or to walk around in order to increase circulation. You'll find your concentration much improved.

Read Extensively.

Superior students are not always rapid readers, but they read extensively, with excellent comprehension. You don't need a high I.Q. to read well. In fact, seventy percent of all poor readers have an average or above-average I.Q. It's necessary to be a good reader because you will get seventy-five percent of all your information from printed material. A useful guideline is this: If your grades are low, the first thing to suspect is poor reading skills. It's not difficult to improve them, provided you seek qualified help. Once you're satisfied with your reading skills, use them. Read as much as you can, and read material with varying levels of difficulty. It's not enough to read the morning newspaper if you want to be really well-read. Read textbooks, non-fiction best sellers, and magazines. The important thing is to read as much as you can.

Use the Habit of Overkill.

Anticipate deadlines and complete papers and projects well in advance. This serves the dual purpose of insuring assignment completion and allowing for the possibility of its review or revision. If your paper is due on the sixteenth, finish it by the tenth or twelfth. Then, if your schedule suddenly gets crowded and hectic, there's no anxieties getting it in on time. And if you get any new ideas, you'll have time to include them in your assignment.

Consider Dreams.

Don't neglect your subconscious mind. A good student studies before sleeping because the mind can use the dream state to rework your material. Many famous inventions have been discovered through dreams. In the subconscious or dream state, your mind can re-sort, re-create, and review material so that it becomes even more powerful and clear the next morning. Study or review immediately before sleeping. Then tell yourself that you wish to dream about it. In time, you'll be literally dreaming your way to success.

Know Your Teacher.

See your teacher after class and develop a friendship if possible. Clear up difficult points from class lectures and give your teacher feedback on lecture material and presentation. Most instructors really appreciate knowing how well their material is coming across.

It's often beneficial to find out what your teacher's preferences are. What is his or her favorite subject or author? At one university, an American Literature professor reportedly never gave *A's* to undergraduates. An ambitious sophomore talked to him after class and found out that his favorite author was Theodore Dreiser. He had prepared his doctoral dissertation on Dreiser. So the student matched strengths, reading and researching as much as he could on Dreiser. The final exam he wrote (on Dreiser, of course) was so interesting to him and well presented that he earned the only *A* in the class. In short, specialize your approach by appealing to what your professor likes. It will not only help your grades, but you will learn much more.

Be Different.

You are a unique person among every other student at school. Use what is different about yourself to your advantage. Do not worry about what your friends think, but rather what concerns *you*. Their goals should necessarily not be your goals, nor do you need to wear the same styles they wear, or act as others do. A true success follows intuition and an individual plan. A success is unlikely to be swayed by other opinions. Don't be afraid to gamble on your own hunches, and don't be afraid to fail. Everyone who has been very successful will tell you that there were many discouraging words and failures along the way. But have the courage and persistence to believe in yourself. You will win and succeed through that belief.

REVIEW THESE POINTS

*Successful Personal Habits
1. Improve your self-image.
2. Rigid schedules are not necessary.
3. Avoid pre-study rituals.
4. Psych yourself up before studying.
5. Develop Concentration.
6. Use visualization techniques.
7. Take an interest in school.
*Successful School Habits
1. Prepare yourself.
2. Attend classes regularly.
3. Be punctual.
4. Choose an appropriate study area.
5. Read extensively.
6. Use the habit of overkill.
7. Consider dreams.
8. Know your teacher.
9. Be different.

Figure 3.
The Study Process

Use this procedure to provide a plan of attack
for study.

BROWSE:
Entire book.
Note vocabulary
       degree of difficulty
       style
       organization

PREPARE:
Assigned section
Note main ideas, charts, diagrams, maps, illustrations,
       formulas, etc., topic sentences, summaries,
       questions.
Write main ideas.

READ:
To understand, not to memorize.
Respond as you read; write after each section, depending
on material.

REVIEW & CHECK:
Notes on chapter. Fill gaps — refresh memory. Make sure
text and notes agree.

RECALL:
Chapter or section, first from memory, then double-check
from notes. Think about your material.

CHAPTER THREE

ATTACK PLAN FOR STUDYING: A NEW APPROACH

"Whatever the mind of man can conceive and believe it can achieve."

Napoleon Hill

An average student has spent over 22,000 hours studying from the time he or she began school through the twelfth grade. This enormous amount of time can be reduced considerably through dynamic study skills. But most students are never really taught how to study. It's a process the schools expect students to learn on their own. And because it is not usually taught, this is the most important chapter in the book for you. This dynamic study process will help you every time you open a textbook from now on. Learn it and use it.

Efficient studying does not simply consist of reading, underlining, and rereading. Your new study process consists of reading, writing, thinking, and recalling. It is based on the layered learning process and actually takes less time than your old method of study. It may 45 seem longer at first, but each step takes less time, and because it is so well structured, you will have better recall at test time. The following is the explosive, sure-fire study process you need!

Study for Straight A's by reading, writing, thinking, and recalling. Time and again students have proved that reading and recalling is much more effective than spending all your time reading and highlighting. The only way to learn the material is to become actively involved in absorbing and integrating it. Study reading is an active process, not a passive one. So get out your texts and some note paper: you're ready to learn!

Prepare for reading by browsing through your texts. Survey to get an overview of the book, turning pages quickly so that you spend about two minutes to gather the information which answers the following questions:

1. What are the main topics?
2. What do I already know about these topics?
3. What special terminology is used to present the topics?
4. What is the author?
5. How is the book organized?
6. How difficult is the material and how difficult is its presentation?

Begin to structure your notes around the design of the book. Decide how much material you wish to learn. Draw a picture of the organization of it. Put the more important information to the left, details to the right.

Leave more room under topics and titles which have more pages involved. Draw these maps and lines before reading to help your mind organize and store the data better. After a chapter or section, go back and add to your notes. Figure 2 provides an illustration of this method.

Preview each assigned chapter. Move quickly, skimming through the chapter much faster than your usual reading rate. Your purpose here is to find out what is important and how it is presented, not to read it. Check all bold-face headings, turning each into a question you will answer later. Copy under the chapter titles, each of the subtitles, and the main ideas. This will only take a few seconds a page, but it will give you important clues to the material and help you to read it faster later on because you will be prepared for new ideas. Look over the visual aids such as maps, charts, diagrams, illustrations, and pictures. That will help you grasp each point quicker. Then read any summaries or questions included at the end of the chapter. Summaries are usually helpful because they include the points the author felt to be most important.

Before proceeding with your study, set two goals. Set a comprehension goal; decide how well you need to know the material. Will you be tested? If so, how thoroughly? Set a time goal for your particular section or chapter based upon how well you need to know it. In easy or familiar material, your goal may be fifteen pages an hour. But whatever your goal, make sure that it is only for one chapter or section - setting lengthy or unrealistic goals only leads to discouragement and failure. By achieving both of these goals, you will speed your study time greatly.

At this stage you should have in your notes the chapter title, subtitles, and all major ideas. You should already know a lot about the material - and you haven't even read it yet!

Read to understand, not to memorize. Now is the time to read the chapter as quickly as you can to understand the ideas. After each page or major idea, go back to your notes and add the supporting details to them. Don't proceed more than a page without writing something down. This is an important key to textbook comprehension and retention. Respond to the material by continually summarizing it in your notes, using your own words. The old way of studying was to read and forget. Get into the habit of reading and responding. You will find even the most boring books become interesting.

Reduce the use of underlining seemingly important thoughts; do not use hi-liter, magic-marker, or felt tip pens. Such a study method:

1. is premature; you are not in a position to judge what is most important until you've read the entire chapter.
2. postpones learning; you may simply color the material, rather than understand it.
3. is permanent; have you ever tried to erase it?
4. gives all material equal weight.
5. distracts; have you tried to read a used book marked with hi-liter?
6. devaluates the book; it ruins the appearance and resale value of the book.

SELECT A PROPER STUDY AREA!

Instead, use a pencil to mark important ideas. Whenever something looks valuable, put a check mark in the margin, just to the side of the passage. It marks what is important, but is not permanent. Later on, during a review, you can re-evaluate your marks and either leave them in place, erase them, or add a second one for emphasis. This system is one of the most valuable tools you can use. Not only is it flexible, but it is quite inexpensive. Continue reading each chapter, marking what is important with a check, and adding to your notes until you are finished.

Review the material. Go back through the chapter and re-read it quickly to refresh your memory. Answer the chapter questions, see relationships, and complete your notes. Look at your notes. Do you now have details to support each main idea? Can you study that chapter from your notes? The answers should be yes. Your goal has been to get the material out of the text into your notes, then into your mind. Textbooks, written by scientists or professors are often wordy and difficult to understand. Put the ideas in your own words and you will learn the material much faster. The following questions can help you evaluate textbooks and other non-fiction works:

1. Do you clearly understand the author's goal? If not, check the preface, foreword, and introduce.
2. Do you understand how the author has presented his material? What do you think is the general method of presentation? What are the main ideas? Minor ones? Check the Table of Contents for these answers.

3. What are the conclusions drawn by the author? Do you agree with them? Why did the author come to those conclusions? If you do not agree, in what areas was the author weak? Were his premises weak or only his conclusions?

4. How would you compare the author with anyone else you may have read? Is the book up to date? What else have you read that either reaffirmed or conflicted with it? In what ways?

5. Now can you relate the text material to class lecture notes?

Think about your notes and recall them. Spend time to integrate and remember your material because it is as important as reading it. If your notes are unclear, try rewriting them, basing your organization around the main ideas. Think about the concepts presented in the chapter and try to explain them in your own words. Practice recalling information with and without your notes. Try to study as much as possible from your notes. They are bound to be more understandable than the text. Do not spend your time reading and re-reading your texts. Your exams are a test of your thinking and recalling abilities, not usually your reading skills. So practice thinking and recalling your notes and the text material. The study process we have just learned demands proof of your effectiveness through organization and recall. It is simple, yet effective. Let's review the five parts.

REVIEW THESE POINTS

*Prepare for reading by browsing through text
1. Copy chapter titles
2. Structure notes
*Preview each assigned chapter
1. Add subtitles and main ideas to notes
2. Set goals
*Read to understand, not to memorize
1. Use pencil check system
2. Add details to notes for each page
*Review the material
1. Fill gaps in notes where needed
2. Answer questions
*Think and recall

Figure 4.
Sample Notes for Chemistry

These notes, based on the format for exact sciences, include subject description, laws, examples, problems to solve, and solution.

Notes, p. 114

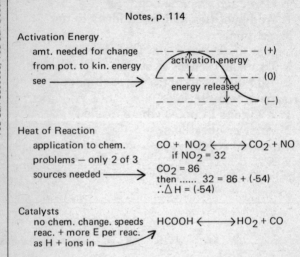

Activation Energy
    amt. needed for change
    from pot. to kin. energy
    see ⟶

Heat of Reaction
    application to chem.
    problems — only 2 of 3
    sources needed ⟶

$$CO + NO_2 \longleftrightarrow CO_2 + NO$$
if $NO_2 = 32$
$CO_2 = 86$
then ...... $32 = 86 + (-54)$
$\therefore \triangle H = (-54)$

Catalysts
    no chem. change. speeds
    reac. + more E per reac.
    as H + ions in ⟶

$$HCOOH \longleftrightarrow HO_2 + CO$$

CHAPTER FOUR

READING FOR RESULTS: SPEED AND COMPRE-HENSION

"Every man who knows how to read has it in his power to magnify himself, to multiply the ways in which he exists, to make his life full, significant, and interesting."
Aldous Huxley

As important as reading is to success in school, many students dislike it. Those who do like to read are usually good at it. A conclusion one might reach is that people like to do things they're good at. This chapter is designed to help you get good at reading so even if you still dislike some of your texts, at least you'll be able to dislike them for less time. This first section is on rapid reading—an essential for success in school.

Most students with poor grades need help in reading skills. Yet, it's no wonder—their last reading lesson was probably in the second grade, and it's unlikely anyone has had a class in comprehension or speed since then. High-powered reading skills can help make school more enjoyable and create plenty of free time. One of the most fascinating areas of learning involves rapid reading skills.

READING FOR SPEED

Would it help you if you could read twice as fast as you presently read? How about twenty times as fast, and with better comprehension? If that sounds impossible, it's not. The human mind is capable of seeing and understanding material as fast as one can turn pages, and some people do read that fast. John Stuart Mill, Teddy Roosevelt, and John F. Kennedy were all naturally fast readers, as have been many others. They were what are known as gifted readers; those who read very fast with excellent comprehension. Gifted readers come from every walk of life, for reading is a skill not related to age, occupation, heredity, or intelligence. The only reason that you may not read fast now is because your natural gifts may have been smothered in school.

The way reading is taught in most public schools is the same technique used a century ago. Curiously, the average American reads at about the same rate today as he read 100 years ago. Most people read between 100 and 400 words per minute, the national average. But slow readers are severely penalized throughout life and are simply unable to keep up because of the tremendous volume of reading required today. Hopefully, schools will change their methods of reading instruction so that someday all students will be rapid readers. In theory, the only things that should decide reading rate are the student's background in the subject, the purpose for reading and ability to turn pages. Some readers have been tested in difficult textbook material who have read thousands of words per minute with excellent comprehension. That's over a dozen pages per minute. Yet some of these super-readers used to read at rates near 200 words per minute! So it is certainly possible for the average reader to increase his or her reading speed considerably.

What does limit your reading rate? Poor habits such as subvocalization (pronouncing words to yourself), regression (going back to re-read material already covered), prolonged fixation (stopping and staring at one word), and inefficient eye movement (losing your place and wandering between lines). These poor habits cause tired eyes, boredom, low speeds, and low comprehension. It is not ability that you lack, it is training. Because we are taught to read at 100-400 words per minute, we are led to believe that is our "normal rate," But those rates are no more normal than 10 or 10,000 words per minute. To improve your rates, it takes proper training and time to replace them with good habits.

A book cannot give the same kind of help that is necessary to make a dramatic increase in your reading skills. Unfortunately, machine speed-reading courses force faster reading without actually breaking the crippling bad habits. The mechanical pacer used with most speed reading machines becomes a crutch which cannot be taken into all reading situations. Several courses actually break the habits causing low speeds and poor comprehension, provided you are willing to spend time working at it. Until you can get some professional help from a well-trained, rapid-reading instructor, there *are* some positive steps you can take.

Read with your hand. As children, we were generally taught not to underline words with our fingertips. But this method actually helps increase speed and comprehension. It builds speed in reading because it prevents unnecessary backing up and re-reading which consumes about one-sixth of your reading time. It also prevents unneeded prolonged fixations, the habit of staring at one word or phrase for a long period. Reading with your hand on the page improves your comprehension because it directs your attention to a spot instead of allowing your eyes and mind to wander. Simply place your fingertip under the first word and move it along at a comfortable rate, underlining each word. Be sure to pick up your finger at the end of each line, lifting it to begin the next one. Read directly above your fingertip and watch your rates soar.

Learn to adjust your rates. Don't read everything at the same rate. You should read light fiction quickly and technical texts at about one-half that rate. When you read easy material, speed up and you will enjoy reading more. A common misconception is that reading faster ruins enjoyment. That is not true.

When you were in first grade, you probably read at a rate of 10-50 words per minute. Now you may read 100-500 words per minute, a full ten times faster! Did you lose any of the enjoyment of books? Of course not, and in fact, you may enjoy books more now than when you read slowly. Decide upon your purpose and read to seek the level of comprehension you require. When your purpose in reading is entertainment, read faster than usual. In a high responsibility situation, take notes often, reread difficult passages, and read at your maximum rate of comprehension, not to memorize.

See yourself as a good reader. Do you see yourself as a slow reader or as a fast reader? Your actions are consistent with your conception of yourself. Always push yourself, being aware of what you need to get out of the material. Believe you can get what you want, when you want it. Seeing yourself as a fast reader can become a self-fulfilling prophecy.

Dr. Maxwell Maltz, author of *Psycho-Cybernetics,* popularized the concept of mental practice, and thousands have used it successfully. He believes each person has a goal-striving mechanism which simply needs to be triggered properly in order to automatically steer a person toward a set goal. What does this mean to you in practical terms? It means that you can "program" yourself to become a better reader, or anything else you like, by using a beautiful built-in success mechanism. This success mechanism is a goal-directed instinct that is easily activated.

Make sure the goal you seek is desirable. Otherwise your internal mechanism may not get the clear signal it needs. Get a strong, clear, and vivid picture of yourself achieving the role you wish. If it's reading improvement you wish, sit back, close your eyes, and picture yourself sitting down at a desk reading rapidly with excellent comprehension. Imagine yourself at a desk or table you know well, moving down the page, not only comprehending what you have read, but quickly recalling it in your notes. Practice this once or twice a day for about two minutes each time. Within several weeks you should see a notable improvement in yourself.

See more words at a time. One reason you might read slowly is that you read with a narrow, constricted, "hard focus"; you have disciplined your eyes to see only a couple of words at a time. This severely limits your speed. Your reading focus is different from your usual vision. The difference is easy to explain. What do you see when you look outside your window? Do your eyes only focus on a spot three-quarters of an inch by five-eighths of an inch? What you see is an entire panorama with everything in focus. You should see a page in the same way.

In order to regain your usual range of vision for reading, you will need some practice. This will require the use of both hands and a large book. Flip through the pages of the book quickly, turning them from the top with your left hand and pulling your eyes down the page by brushing down each page with the edge of your right hand. Your fingers should be extended and relaxed. Follow your hand down each page with your eyes, trying to see as many words as possible. Start by brushing each page in two or three seconds, gradually reducing the time spent on each page until you can go as fast as you can turn pages. Pace yourself, starting at twenty pages a minute, slowly increasing to one hundred pages a minute within one to two months. This practice work helps your eyes see more words at a time by preventing zooming in or focusing only on individual words. Practice for five minutes a day for several weeks. Remember that it is unlikely that you'll read faster without practicing. Reading is a skill, and as with any skill, all the instruction in the world won't help you unless you actually practice what you learn. It's important to learn to see more words at a time. Just those few minutes a day of practice will help prevent missing words.

Some students are afraid that if they go faster, they'll miss words. But they already know most of the words they're about to see. There are over 600,000 words in our language, but 400 of them comprise sixty-five percent of printed material. These are structure words which have no meaning, but they tie the sentence together. For example, in the second sentence of this paragraph, the structure words are: *but, of, the, about, to.* Remove those words and the sentence is choppy, but still readable: "they already know most words they are see." Since you've read those 400 words many times, don't let them slow down your reading by dwelling on them.

A famous psychologist, James Cattell, determined through research that our untrained visual capacity is about four words in one-hundreth of a second. That's 400 words a second or 24,000 words per minute that we're capable of seeing and understanding. Australian psychologist John Ross has reported that the human mind can process depth information in .0002 seconds. He defines depth information as non-fiction technical material. Some students may wonder whether or not they can comprehend material by reading at a faster rate. Accept the fact you can. Just practice at it and you'll see results immediately.

Don't worry about understanding everything when you read fast. You can see and understand everything, but merely reading something does not insure retention. You'll retain information by practicing recall, not by reading slower. Usually the slower you read, the more the mind wanders, with little comprehension and recall.

The ideal level on which to read is a purely mental or intellectual plane. This means don't clog or block information in your mind by negative emotions such as anxiety, worrying, and fear of "not getting it." If you develop an open, positive, "go-for-it" attitude, you'll read much better.

At higher rates of speed it's also helpful to talk to yourself. Discuss out loud the topic of each paragraph for additional clarity and reinforcement. Conceptual vocalization, the skill of thinking out loud, enables you to better process ideas and concepts.

In order to get the comprehension you need at faster speeds, it helps to have an adequate background in the material. You can get background information in several ways: 1) from reading other material on that subject, 2) personal experience, 3) from pre reading. The purpose of pre-reading is to become familiar with the main ideas and to organize those ideas into a pattern. This organizing step is crucial in developing speed in reading textbook material.

One other hint which will help you read fast is often overlooked: hold your book four to six inches *further* away from your eyes than usual. Your eyes won't have to work so hard because the farther things are from your eyes, the less movement it takes to see them all. So be sure your material is at least fifteen inches from your eyes; you'll enjoy increased speed, and comprehension, and reduce fatigue.

READING FOR COMPREHENSION

Readers with the best comprehension are usually fast readers. The slower you read, the more chances there are for you to daydream and lose concentration, hence, comprehension. Getting good comprehension is a process and a habit, not a mystery. Actually, comprehension is a two-fold process: 1) perceiving and organizing information, and, 2) relating that information to what you already know.

Several factors determine the degree of comprehension you'll get from the material you read. Those factors are your background in that subject, your reading skills and the organization and presentation of that material.

There is virtually no comprehension when the reader does not have the necessary vocabulary and background. Comprehension is largely dependent on how well the reader already knows the subject. Because background increases the vocabulary and subject familiarity, get the most amount of prior knowledge you can. Then processing becoming almost subliminal, it happens so fast. When the reader has an extensive background, there is even a point at which material can be read prior to conscious awareness. Background is the reason why a beginning law student might read at 70 to 200 words per minute, yet a practicing attorney can read the same material much faster. Therefore, the first habit to get into that will build comprehension is gain the necessary background for that subject. Two excellent ways to accomplish this are listening to lectures and reading other easier material on the same subject.

Read actively for greater meaning. Reading is an active process not a passive one. Anticipate ideas and read for a purpose to answer your questions by actively searching for the information you want. Have questions in mind before you read, not afterwards. If you begin reading a book with questions, you'll complete your reading with the answers. Think about the important points and read to understand them. Be confident that you can get what you want and you will. Don't argue with the author while reading. Save critical analysis for later so you will not slow yourself down, lose concentration, and miss the flow of the material. Put a pencil check in the margin of areas you would like to go back to.

Read to understand, not to memorize. In order to have a smooth, continuous flow of information to your mind, don't stop to memorize facts. Save that process for later when you study your notes. Read a page, summarize the data in your notes, then continue. At all times you should read as rapidly as you can understand the ideas.

Maintain proper attitude and desire. You must care about what you are reading or studying. If you don't, create a need to care. Use positive reinforcement. You might say to yourself, "Once I get this reading done, I'll be able to go do something I enjoy more. Don't use negative reinforcement or a self-threat such as, "If I don't get an *A* in this class, I'll lose my scholarship." If you maintain a strong, receptive attitude, you will find comprehension will be easier because you are not fighting yourself. Fighting reading is much like panicing while swimming. The secret is to relax.

Upgrade poor physical habits. It's difficult to comprehend what you read when you are tired, sleepy, depressed, or in pain. Some students complain that their comprehension is poor while doing their reading at three in the morning. At that hour, many couldn't comprehend the morning newspaper. It is critical to be not only alert, but relaxed. Be comfortable and tune with the subject of the book. Reading posture definitely affects comprehension. Sit at a desk when possible. Study in an upright position with the book flat on the table, fifteen or more inches away. The more stretched out and relaxed your study position, the more you will encourage its usual result - drowsiness, poor concentration, or sleep. If you want comprehension, speed, and retention, sit up alertly, and act like you are serious about accomplishing the task.

Use the layered learning process. The study procedure described in the previous chapter is an extremely useful tool for comprehension. Basically it involves approaching the material on several levels, and taking notes after each. As a review, here are the steps: 1) Browse through the material, becoming aware of its structure, complexity, and organization; 2) prepare and preview the material more slowly, noting bold-face headings, summaries, subtitles, visual aids and topic sentences. Add main ideas to your notes. Set your purpose - exactly what level of comprehension do you need? How far away is the exam? With your purpose in mind, set a realistic chapter or section goal. 3) Read the material, a chapter at a time, moving as quickly as you can understand the ideas. Stop after each page and add details to your main ideas. 4) Review your notes and text, filling in gaps, viewing the overall content and organization, and refreshing your memory. 5) Think about and recall the information.

Organize what you read. Your mind seeks organization, logical sequences, and order. Give it a chance to comprehend the material by grouping ideas and details into meaningful blocks. Restructure the material into easy-to-picture thoughts. Use every possible combination of thought-pictures that will work. When you perceive the unity and structure of the material you are studying you will grasp its meaning much faster. Strive toward understanding the structure as well as the details.

Write as you read. Get in the habit of recalling on paper immediately what you have read. Because you will understand each point better, the following point will be that much clearer. Comprehension depends upon understanding each preceding idea. The better you understand and recall one idea, the more likely you will understand the next. Stick to each part of the study process and you will find comprehension becoming a habit.

REVIEW THESE POINTS

*Read for Speed
  1. Realize that there is no limit to your speed
  2. Read with your hand
  3. Learn to adjust your rates according to material and purpose

4. See your self as a good reader
5. See more words at a time
*Read for Comprehension
1. Read quickly to improve concentration
2. Read actively for greater meaning
3. Read to understand, not to memorize
4. Maintain good attitude and desire
5. Upgrade poor physical habits
6. Use the layered learning process
7. Organize what you read
8. Write as you read

READ WITH YOUR HAND!

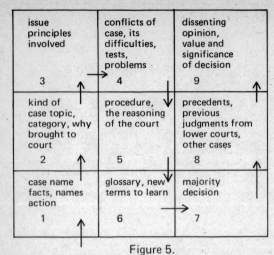

Figure 5.

Sample Notes for Law Texts

This format helps organize a law case quickly and clearly. While a third-year law student would look for a different approach than a first-year student, the basic information is the same.

CHAPTER FIVE

NOTES THAT SPARKLE: THE KIND OF NOTES YOU'LL LOVE TO STUDY

"First we raise the dust, then we claim we cannot see."

Berkeley

Efficient notes are vital to straight *A's*. Most of your studying should be done from notes taken in class and from the text. Your notes show how well you understand the material presented. Students are not usually taught how to take concise, creative notes. Most have to learn from others or through trial and error. Learn the following basics for general usage. Then use your creativity to develop some formats that work best for you and the subjects in which you are interested.

Make sure your notes represent the material, not duplicate the text. Your notes should not be a re-creation, but rather a synopsis, a synthesis. Accuracy is your first consideration. But beyond that, try to reconstruct the material in your own words. That is the beauty of good notes; they are more understandable and interesting than a text or lecture. Include as many examples as time or necessity permits.

Devise your own shorthand. It is time-consuming to spell out each word you choose to include in your notes. You can phonetically abbreviate by using the consonants of a word to create a phonetic representation which you will be able to write rapidly and interpret easily upon review. Look at the following sentence from a lecture given in a literature class:

Jean-Paul Sartre is a French existentialist who was born in Paris in 1905.

Your notes might read as follows:

Sartre, exis, Paris 1905.

Use as many symbols and abbreviations from math as you can. Table 1 shows some symbols which can be used for cuts in note-taking.

Vary the size of titles and headings. The thoughts and ideas you record will not all be of the same importance. With some practice, you will begin to automatically write more important ideas in larger size print and details much smaller. Such variations will help you remember your notes more easily, and make them more fun to take down. Another method that is helpful is the use of geometric shapes to identify and categorize ideas. Table 2 shows some examples.

Learn the basic format of the subject. Each subject group has basic characteristics which help you organize information and your thoughts on that particular subject. Many students are stumped in notetaking because in some textbooks the information on each page is not well-organized. Some books may go for a dozen pages without bold-face headings or changes in organization. Difficulty often occurs in studying and taking notes from such textbooks. Fortunately, most textbooks are better written today then they were years ago. Many have chapter summaries, bold-face headings, and questions to answer. But when you use a book which does not indicate what is important by its format, use the information in Table 3 to help organize your notes and study procedure. Table 3 includes the basic formats for three main subject areas.

In order to take notes well, you must be proficient at sorting information. To understand an idea, you need to see its parts as well as its whole. Depending on the subject, the parts are quite predictable. First, find the main idea; it is often in the first two sentences of each paragraph. To do that, look for phrases like "most importantly," "first of all," "it must be emphasized that ..." Any similar phrase is the author's way of telling you that something important is being said.

Second, find supporting details and examples to explain the main ideas. These usually follow the main idea and often include stories or data, such as names and dates.

Next, isolate the information you will need by sorting actual facts from filler data such as the author's personal experiences and opinions. This is easy because the facts are often proper names, places, or numbers. Once isolated from the facts, the remaining material can often be identified as filler.

Texts often follow a sequence. For example, math texts might follow this sequence: Background information, statement of laws, axioms, or theorems, examples, problems presented to be solved. When you take notes for a math class, don't simply copy an important theorem. Ensure comprehension by examining the other parts of the sequence of information.

Use a creative approach, not the standard outline form. The more unusual and eye-catching your notes are, the more likely you will enjoy studying them and be able to recall them. Use pictures, cartoons, arrows, different colored pens, and different size headings. Don't use the standard outline form except as a last resort. Its two major drawbacks are inflexibility and difficulty in recalling. Helpful, creative notes take very little practice, but if you need some ideas, refer to Figures 4-9.

Keep class lecture notes and text study notes together. An ingenious way to learn a subject quickly and with better understanding is to take notes in tandem. Take class lecture notes on a page opposite the notes you took while studying the text.

Ideally, you should read the text and take notes prior to the class lecture. Put your notes on the left-hand side of your paper, leaving the right-half for class work. Then when the professor lectures, you will not only under-

stand his comments better, but you won't have to write as much. If you keep class and text notes on the same topic together on a page, you will take fewer notes and understand more. Other students in class may be writing frantically while you relax and only jot down an occasional supporting detail. Even if you can't take text notes in advance, bring your lecture notes home and reverse the process.

REVIEW THESE POINTS

*Notetaking skills
1. Make sure your notes represent the material, not duplicate the text
2. Devise your own shorthand
3. Vary the size of titles and headings
4. Learn the basic format of the subject

5. Use a creative approach, not the standard outline form
6. Keep class lecture notes and text study notes together
7. Review Tables 1-4 and Figures 4-9

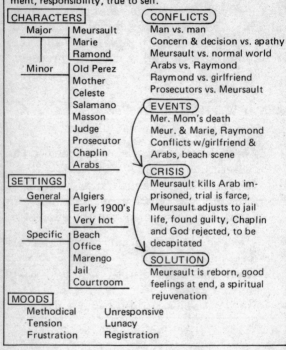

THE STRANGER, by Albert Camus

AUTHOR 1913-60, Fr. existentialist, Nobel Prize '57.
Works inc. THE FALL, THE PLAGUE, THE REBEL.
Believed in decisions, you are what you do, action, commitment, responsibility, true to self.

CHARACTERS

Major	Meursault
	Marie
	Ramond
Minor	Old Perez
	Mother
	Celeste
	Salamano
	Masson
	Judge
	Prosecutor
	Chaplin
	Arabs

SETTINGS

General	Algiers
	Early 1900's
	Very hot
Specific	Beach
	Office
	Marengo
	Jail
	Courtroom

MOODS

Methodical	Unresponsive
Tension	Lunacy
Frustration	Registration

CONFLICTS

Man vs. man
Concern & decision vs. apathy
Meursault vs. normal world
Arabs vs. Raymond
Raymond vs. girlfriend
Prosecutors vs. Meursault

EVENTS

Mer. Mom's death
Meur. & Marie, Raymond
Conflicts w/girlfriend &
Arabs, beach scene

CRISIS

Meursault kills Arab imprisoned, trial is farce,
Meursault adjusts to jail
life, found guilty, Chaplin
and God rejected, to be
decapitated

SOLUTION

Meursault is reborn, good
feelings at end, a spiritual
rejuvenation

Figure 6.
Sample Notes for Novels

This format includes background on author, characters, settings, problems, events, crises, and solutions.

CHAPTER SIX

USING YOUR MEMORY MORE EFFECTIVELY: DRAWING MENTAL PICTURES

"I'll never forget what's his name."
Norman Pliscou

Harry Lorayne, a well-known memory whiz, once memorized the first 300 pages of the Manhattan telephone directory. Although this feat included over 30,000 names and numbers, he is the first to admit it's not difficult! Memory is an abstraction or process, not an organ. So when we say someone has a good memory, what we really mean is that they are good at memory skills. The activity or skill of remembering can be improved in the same way the skill at chess or tennis can. This is good news! You are not stuck with a poor memory. The reasons that cause poor memory skills can be identified, and steps can be taken to improve memory.

WHY WE FORGET

Negative Thinking.

Many of us reinforce our lack of recall so often it makes it difficult to remember. For example, how often have you heard, "I'm awful with names," or "I can never remember numbers,"? All this habit does is to encourage the mind not to even try to remember. After all, the excuse has already been given for failure. Don't downplay any part of your memory. It only encourages mental blocks. The first step in improving memory is to believe you can, and eliminate negative thoughts about your ability to do so.

A Weak Impression.

It's very easy to forget something which never made a strong impression on you to begin with. This could stem from one or more of the following:

1. Not paying attention to the idea
2. Not thinking the idea was important
3. Not having or taking the time to learn the idea

Disuse.

Much like a muscle in the body, you must use your memory in order for it to function at its best. German psychologist Hermann Ebbinghaus studied memory skills and discovered some remarkable statistics. He found that on the average, we forget seventy percent of what we've learned in one hour, and we forget a whopping eighty-four percent within forty-eight hours. These figures are based on no usage of memory after initial learning. You can see that disuse of memory is devastating.

Interference.

A poor learning situation during a memory activity or static and confusing situations afterwards can cause memory interference. For example, it is not a good idea to try to study geometry immediately after algebra. Your memory will be confused by similar figures and symbols. Accordingly, it would be difficult to memorize a Shakespeare play followed by Dryden's poetry. It's also more difficult to remember things when followed by a period of excitement or emotional intensity. For example, it is not recommended that you go straight from studying history to a homecoming football game. Your mind would experience too much interference for easy recall.

Repression.

Repression, the act of excluding something from your consiousness, develops as a result of mental blocks that we consciously or unconsciously set up. Most of us have repressed negative events from our childhood. Unfortunately, this same ability to "bury" things grows with us, and we find ourselves repressing desired information, too. These mental blocks were set up originally as protection from unnecessary emotional trauma. Try to make sure you don't repress information that is really needed.

STEPS TO BETTER RECALL

1. Pay Attention.

Being aware is the first step to developing better recall. Begin to notice the part of the page on which information is located. Notice how it's presented and take an extra look at visual aids. Surprisingly, many people do not even know such basic things as what color their walls and curtains are, what their license plate number is, or even their social security number. Knowing these things may not be very important, but by learning to be more aware of your surroundings can be very helpful in developing memory skills.

2. Get the Information Right.

Make sure that you correctly understand the data. This sounds like a simple rule, but particularly in the case of remembering statistics, people rarely focus on the numbers themselves. They pay attention to the significance of them. At gatherings where new people are introduced, make sure you understand the name and its spelling. Then repeat it to the person for clarification and reinforcement.

3. Tell Yourself you Can.

Telling yourself you can remember is part of developing a healthy self-image. Faith in yourself relaxes and encourages stronger mental processes through opening previously closed thought channels. We can only do what we believe we can.

4. Develop Desire.

Most of the time, the incentive to remember information is already there. But every object of memory is made much stronger when you intensify your desire to recall. If you met someone at a party who interested you, your desire to remember their name and phone number would be strong. Similarly, when you know you'll be tested on a book, your efforts increase appreciably.

5. Understand.

Though it may sound obvious, make sure you understand thoroughly what you want to remember. This rule applies equally to poetry, mathematics, history, sciences, and related fields. If something makes sense, it's much easier to recall.

6. Be Creative.

One of the most powerful ways to recall is to unleash your imagination. Turn your text material into pictures, change names into pictures, exaggerate, and be artistic. Try to put some color into the data; associate sight, sound, taste and smell with it.

7. Use Repetition.

Immediately after a learning activity, preferably within an hour, refresh your memory through a review. We use both a long-term and short-term memory and most of what we take in goes into our short-term memory. For example, when you look up a number in the phone book, you remember it just long enough to dial it. Then you'll promptly forget it. That's of course, short-term. To get data transferred to our long-term recall, we need to repeat it and use it for reinforcement. The ideal way to study and memorize is to spend six one-hour sessions on a subject, rather than six straight hours. In this way data is reinforced sufficiently to be put into our long-term memory.

8. Create Mental Pictures.

Often called the key to memorizing, mental pitures enable your mind to work in its more natural state. Usually, your mind stores images and pictures, not words. When you think of milk, do you picture the four letters *m-i-l-k?* Most people picture a glass or carton of milk. By the normal storage system, by creating mental pictures, you can remember data much more easily. Change words and ideas into pictures and simply study the pictures, not the words. There are several books in the bibliography on memory and mental pictures which are helpful. Many of these even show how to turn numbers and equations into pictures.

9. Learn the Technique of Association.

Probably the simplest method of remembering is by association, the process of recalling one item because another reminded you of it. This system requires no more than some awareness and a quick mental picture. For example, if you wanted to remember to bring a pen to class, simply imagine black, gooey ink

GET THE INFORMATION RIGHT!

all over the door knob where you live. Make a quick, but strong mental picture of it. Then when you leave for class, reaching for the door knob will trigger the mental picture of ink, and you'll remember your pen.

10. Practice Recall Under all Conditions.

If you practice recalling only under "prime" conditions, information may elude you during test time. When you have critical information to remember, create flash cards on 3×5-inch index cards to take with you. Then whenever you have a break, at mealtime, while relaxing, or in the library, study the cards and practice recalling.

11. Study Contrasting Subjects.

Apparently our subconscious needs time to sort and categorize information for long-term storage and retrival. To facilitate this process, do not study two similar subjects back to back. Instead, work on a dissimilar subject in between. For example, do not follow the study of algebra with calculus or Spanish with Italian.

12. Reduce Interference.

Cut down on distractions which might ordinarily follow a study session. It is best to study before a restful, quiet time or even before bed. Then your mind will have time to relax, sort, and store the necessary information.

13. Study Wholes, not Just Parts.

Whether the subject is a Shakespearean play or an assignment in anatomy, our mind functions best with complete pictures to remember. Even if you have to memorize only one part of a chapter, become familiar with the all of it. For example, if you had to explain to someone why a local beach has low and high tides, it would be much easier if you also discussed how our tides are simply opposite those on the other side of the world. For some reason our recall even varies within the whole picture we are learning. Use the B.E.M. concept for better recall also. We remember material best from the beginning, second best from the end, and our recall is weakest on the middle. Therefore spend more time on the middle to allow for that tendency.

14. Practice Using the Material.

Frequently review, repeat, recite, and use the material you wish to remember. Almost any information learned becomes familiar, and even second nature, through usage. Try to integrate the data into daily usage. There is no substitute for practice.

PRACTICING MENTAL PICTURES

Learn to link one word to another in order to form associations. Your memory skills will improve if you practice creating mental pictures about what you want to recall. The more unusual and absurd the mental picture you create, the more likely you will be to recall the word or information you associated with it. Use the following ideas to create vivid mental pictures:

1. Imagine some kind of *action* taking place.
2. Form an image which is *out of proportion*.
3. Create in your mind an *exaggerated version* of the subject.
4. Substitute and *reverse* a normal role.
   For example, in order to remember to mail a letter, imagine the letter carrying *you* out to the mailbox and stuffing *you* inside.

Improve your memory skills by practicing word associations using mental pictures. For example, in associating the words *table* and *dance,* first form a clear picture of a table in your mind. Visualize a table that you use frequently, one which is familiar to you. In order to associate *table* with *dance,* imagine the table standing up on two legs, dancing wildly, with the other two legs spinning in the air. Because it is such an absurd picture, it will stick in your mind. Each time you think of table, you will think of dance.

Linking of words can continue in a similar manner. If you wished to next link the word *dance* to *duck,* for example, you might create a mental picture of a huge, six-foot-tall, all white, overfed, pot-bellied duck dancing and whirling, with feathers flying.

Using the method of linking through mental pictures, you have created a chain of associations: *table* to *dance, dance* to *duck.* In this way, you never try to memorize more than one word at a time. The process is all done with mental pictures. The system of forming associations by using the link method will help you to memorize lists of names, places, events, items, or almost anything. Table 5 includes additional ideas on how to use association.

REVIEW THESE POINTS

*Why We Forget
   1. Negative thinking
   2. A weak impression
   3. Disuse
   4. Interference
   5. Repression
*Steps to Better Recall
   1. Pay attention
   2. Get the information right
   3. Tell yourself you can
   4. Develop desire
   5. Understand
   6. Be creative
   7. Use repetition
   8. Create mental pictures
   9. Learn the technique of association
   10. Practice recall under all conditions
   11. Study contrasting subjects
   12. Reduce interference
   13. Study wholes, not just parts
   14. Practice using the material

USING MENTAL PICTURES!

1. PICTURE A TABLE.
2. IMAGINE IT DANCING.
3. DANCING WITH A HUGE DUCK.
4. WALNUTS ARE RAINING ON THE DUCK.
5. A WALNUT IS CAUGHT BETWEEN YOUR TOES.
6. ON YOUR TOES, YOU SEE A MIRROR INSTEAD OF A TOENAIL.
7. IN THE MIRROR, YOU SEE A BEAR.
8. THE BEAR IS IN A CANOE.
9. THE CANOE IS ATTACHED TO A NECKLACE.
10. THE NECKLACE CATCHES ON FIRE.

THE CIVIL WAR

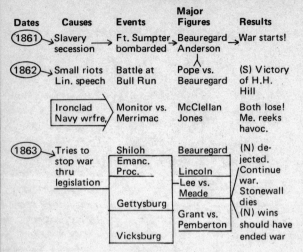

Dates	Causes	Events	Major Figures	Results
1861	Slavery secession	Ft. Sumpter bombarded	Beauregard Anderson	War starts!
1862	Small riots Lin. speech	Battle at Bull Run	Pope vs. Beauregard	(S) Victory of H.H. Hill
	Ironclad Navy wrfre.	Monitor vs. Merrimac	McClellan Jones	Both lose! Me. reeks havoc.
1863	Tries to stop war thru legislation	Shiloh / Emanc. Proc. / Gettysburg / Vicksburg	Beauregard / Lincoln / Lee vs. Meade / Grant vs. Pemberton	(N) dejected. Continue war. Stonewall dies (N) wins should have ended war

Figure 7.
Sample Notes for History

Categorize your information so that you will follow the flow of events better. This format allows a better understanding of details as well as major events.

CHAPTER SEVEN

WORD POWER: VOCABULARY, SPELLING, LIBRARY AIDS

"Words are the ammunition of the mind."
Bill Ballance

If you think a good vocabulary would help you get straight *A's,* you are right. In nearly every field, the successful person also has a powerful vocabulary. Scholars believe a good vocabulary is so important that it is a major part of any IQ test. Students with an effective vocabulary excel not only in English, but also in math, science, and business. And the reason they excel is not because they are any smarter, but because they can better express themselves. In almost any business in the country, the higher an employee's position, the better his working vocabulary. Yet, how can you improve your vocabulary?

Become well-read. Many periodicals are written for people with a sixth-grade education. In order to improve your vocabulary, subscribe to newspapers and magazines of high journalistic quality. Some excellent publications are Harper's, The Nation, Intellectual Digest, Psychology Today, and The New Yorker. Reading material of this caliber will help you learn many new words.

Develop interest in new words. Use the dictionary to learn new or unfamiliar words. Jot down definitions on a notepad that you keep posted. Refer to it often to refresh your memory. Use new words as often as possible, even to the point of overuse. Try to learn a new word each week. You will be amazed at how quickly your vocabulary increases. The only valid way to add new words to your daily vocabulary is by consciously interjecting them in conversation until you feel comfortable using them.

Associate with people who have good vocabularies. Expressive, articulate speakers have a way of influencing others. Their ability to express themselves will encourage your use of new words. Your level of communication varies with the people with whom you converse. A college graduate has to simplify language in order to explain how a president is elected when talking to a first grader. But the same person may actually use more difficult and specialized terminology when talking to a professor at school. Associating with people who have a good command of the English language will help to elevate your level of communication and improve your vocabulary.

READ, READ, READ, READ!

Take a Latin or Greek class. The English language evolved from many languages, but a large percent of the words in our dictionary have a Latin or Greek origin. At a high school, college, or through community adult education programs, you can enroll in a class which gives a superlative background to word origins and definitions. You may be surprised how much this helps.

Get in the dictionary and thesaurus habit. Whenever you come across a word which is unfamiliar to you or which you don't understand, turn to the dictionary. It is the good speller who uses the dictionary, not the poor one. Get in the habit of referring to the dictionary, regardless of whether you are reading a newspaper or a scholarly journal. The most important thing to remember when looking up definitions of new words is not to stop there. Make use of new words in your daily conversation every chance you get.

A thesaurus is another useful book for learning the meanings of words. A thesaurus is a dictionary of synononyms. For each entry in a thesaurus, many words which have the same or similar meanings are listed. For example, *Roget's Thesaurus* lists twenty-nine synonyms for the word expert, including master, medalist, genius, mastermind, prodigy, first fiddle, and connoisseur. A thesaurus is more complete in its definitions and a lot of fun to use. Browse through one, and you may find words much more interesting.

Improve your spelling. Start noticing how words are spelled when you read. Take a course in grammar or composition. Respond to class feedback; when your papers are returned to you, notice the spelling corrections. Sometimes it helps to have another person to review your assignments. Pay attention to phonetic sounds, and listen carefully to how words are pronounced. A large percentage of the words in our language are spelled just the way they sound.

Three good ways to sharpen your spelling ability are to learn roots, suffixes, and prefixes. Root words build both spelling and comprehension skills. Table 6 lists ten common roots. Learning them will instantly bring understanding of hundreds of words to your fingertips. The appendix provides some spelling rules. Review them and commit them to memory. Some of the most commonly misspelled, misused words appear in table 7. Study the table to avoid confusing words that are spelled similarly or pronounced the same.

Achieve success in the library. The true master of words goes to the library often. A library does not have to be confusing and intimidating. Check to see if a library guide is published by your school. You gain specific information on how to check out books, which books are on time limit, which ones can not be checked out, and library hours.

Basically, there are three main sources of information in a library. First, there are reference books which include dictionaries, encyclopedias, almanacs, and other materials which can usually be checked out. The reference librarian can be very helpful to you when you need to locate exact data in reference materials.

The second main source of information is magazines, journals, and periodicals. There are several reference books which list information and its location in a periodical by subject, author, and titles. Check the *Reader's Guide to Periodical Literature* for most general subjects, the *International Index to Periodicals* for scientific articles, and *Poole's Index to Periodical Literature* for materials published during the 19th century. There are also specific indexes for the New York Times, psychology, poetry, drama, education and other fields. The librarian can help you find those easily.

The third and most commonly used source of information is non-fiction books and novels. To find these quickly, you can use the Dewey Decimal System of Classification and the card catalogue. The Dewey Decimal System is a method of organizing books by subject area. It includes ten categories with numbers assigned for each. Here's the system:

000-099 General Works: autobiographies

100-199 Philosophy: psychology, ethics, logic

200-299 Religion: theology, the Bible

300-399 Social Sciences: economics, political science, sociology

400-499 Philology: languages

500-599 Sciences: chemistry, physics, mathematics

600-699 Applied Sciences: medicine, agriculture, engineering, biology

700-799 Arts: architecture, painting, crafts

800-899 Literature: world, American, ancient and present

900-999 History: biographies

All the books which fall under a specific category are located on the library shelves with the corresponding number. For example, *Alice in Wonderland,* a novel by Lewis Carroll, would be located somewhere on the shelves marked 800-899. But if you were trying to find that book, instead of searching the entire 800-899 section, you could consult the card catalogue to determine the specific number and thereby save time.

The card catalogue is the "brain" of the library and it has three parts. You can use any one of the three indexes to help you find the location of a particular source. The first possibility is an author index which indicates where you can find all works published by a particular author that the library carries. Another part of the card catalogue is a title index. There you can find the location of a book as long as you know its title. Finally, if you know neither an author's name nor the book title, you can consult the subject index. There you'll find book titles listed under each main idea or subject you choose. So actually, a book could be listed in all three parts of the card catalogue. The book *Psycho-Cybernetics* would be listed under its own title, the author Maxwell Maltz, and the subject of psychology.

Make the library work for you. Most successful students make good use of it for both work and play. The library has so many sections that it may take many visits to completely investigate all it offers. But once you have learned how to use the library and feel at home with it, you've added a valuable asset to your student life.

REVIEW THESE POINTS

Word Power
1. Importance of strong vocabulary
2. Become well-read
3. Develop interest in new words
4. Associate with people who have good vocabularies
5. Take a Greek or Latin class
6. Use the dictionary and thesaurus
7. Improve your spelling
8. Achieve success in the library

BACKGROUND ON ARTIST
    Current society is ?
    Scien-philos-astron-
    "A is A,"concretes,
    the realistic, specifics
 	
A's ANALYSIS OF S.C.
    (−) pop. mngmnt.
    (−) laws
        property laws
    bribes $
    no election of ovrsrs
    (−) treasury low on $
    (+) excess lifetime offcrs
    (+) must add soldiers
 	
(Q's FOR CLASS)
    implications of his crit.
    justified?
    Compr/contr w/US
     Constit.
    define "polis"
           "Ephoralty"	

Figure 8.
Sample Notes for Philosophy

In these notes, the left-hand side was prepared in advance, from the texts. Then the page of notes is taken to the class lecture so that additional comments can be made on the right-hand side.

CHAPTER EIGHT

EVALUATING BOOKS: BE AN INSTANT CRITIC

*"Daring as it is to investigate the unknown,
even more so is it to question the known."*
                                                    Kaspar

Students are often asked to evaluate books in school. But the skills necessary for assessing a work of fiction are not usually taught in most schools. The many levels of meaning of novels, plays, and poems don't have to elude all but the sharpest students. All it takes is a method of approach, and your desire to follow it through.

Prepare for reading. Get together your fiction work, note paper, and prepare to write. Before you start reading, look at the front and back covers, the preface, and foreword. Then browse through the book to learn the following:

1. how the book is structured—length of chapters, parts, or acts
2. who the characters are and where the story takes place (proper names and nouns will be easy to spot, so write them down)

3. how the title is related to the story.

You should have a few notes on the story before you begin reading.

Meet the author. Every fiction work is an interpretation of some aspect of life as seen through the eyes of the author. Get to know that person and you'll gain insight into what he or she writes about and why. The four best ways to meet an author are:

1. Ask your instructor for information on the author's life.
2. Read other works by the same author.
3. Check the book's jacket, introduction, preface, or publisher's notes.
4. Find a biography or autobiography of the author and learn as much as you can.

Organize the information. Comprehension and meaning come quickly when the story has unity and flows well. Try to discover the flow of ideas by organizing the information you have recorded into categories. Use the format illustrated in Figure 10 to organize your notes about characters, setting, moods, conflicts, events, complications, crises, and solutions.

The list of characters should include a comment about each of the major ones and a listing of the minor ones. Usually there is one general setting, and many more specific ones, so list them in sequence. For moods, write down how the characters feel about their positions in the action of the story, as well as how you react to each character. Is it light fiction, a horror story, a mystery, or a satire?

To analyze events, crises, and solutions, record happenings of importance in the plot, and the events which led to the crisis or turning point, when things have gone about as far as they can go. Suddenly, the pressure is released, and momentum switches. A major decision is reached, the crisis is resolved, and the remainder of the story is usually a winding-down. Sometimes the author's solutions and viewpoints are presented in these last pages of the novel. By organizing your information around these elements of the plot the different levels of meaning will surface quickly, and your understanding of the novel will increase.

Ask questions before and after reading. The list of questions which follow are designed to help you understand what the author is saying, how he or she says it, and why. They are fairly easy to answer if you review the list before you do your reading. Your mind then will be more alert, subconciously seeking the answers to each question. Most students gather enough information to evaluate fiction; they just need a way to derive qualitative, meaningful data from it. Use the following questions to help you evaluate fiction:

Ask yourself what the author's goal is. Why did he or she write the book (to inform, persuade, entertain, etc.)? Did the author successfully meet this goal? How did the book affect you? Could it have been more effective?

Then look for problems and conflicts. What kind of conflicts are presented? Conflicts include man *vs.* man, man *vs.* nature, and man *vs.* himself. Are they solved? How? How do you feel about the solution? Is it realistic?

Toward which characters does the author seem to feel most sympathetic and why? Do they represent a political, social, economic, or moral viewpoint? Which one? Are the characters convincing in their role? Were they believable, or supposed to be believable?

What changes do the characters go through in the book? Did they change for the better or for the worse? What caused the change? What do the changes represent?

Who was the main character in the novel? Does the main character represent the viewpoint of the author? What does the main character believe in? How do you feel about the main character? Why? How does the character meet his or her goals, or are these goals met?

On what does the author base the book? A historical situation or changing social trend? A recent disaster, politics, or inventions? How does this book fit into literature in general, or current historical perspective? Could it have been written more smoothly? Did the book have impact? Would you recommend it to others?

Learn ways to criticize an author's work. The more you read, the better equipped you will be to analyze and critique fiction. If you want to critique Hemingway's *Farewell to Arms,* there are several approaches you might choose. You might decide to compare it with his other major works. For example, you might read *The Sun Also Rises* and contrast it to *Farewell To Arms.* To be able to judge Hemingway's style, you might decide to study a variety of writing styles as typified by American authors Fitzgerald, Faulkner, Mailer, or Vonnegut.

Examine the author's objective? Is the author trying to inform, entertain, persuade, criticize, or merely sell books? Did the author succeed? Was the dialogue meant to be realistic, and is it? What is the tone of the novel - sarcasm, realism, hope, despair? Is it effective? How long does the author spend on crucial sequences of events as compared with minor events?

Analyze the characters. How are they introduced? Are any introduced and then forgotten? Why? Are the characters consistent in their behavior, or were they meant to be otherwise? Do the conversations fit each character's portrayal? Or do they contradict it? Which character does the author favor and why?

Determine the author's writing style and mechanics. Are any parts of the books so wordy that the plot suffers? Is all of the narration necessary? Is the sentence structure varied? How does the author balance main ideas with minor ideas? Does the author keep you interested by creating a desire to continue reading? Do you react the way the characters do? Are you swept into the action? Does the book have a single unifying direction or theme?

Ascertain the author's viewpoint. What philosophies does the author seem to put forth? Does the book reflect the beliefs of Plato, Aristotle, existentialism, realism, or naturalism? At any point is the author illogical, misinformed, prejudiced, incomplete, incorrect, or inconsistent? How do the author's ideas fit into today's thinking? Is the story believable? Was it meant to be? Does the title fit the story?

There is practically an endless list of criteria by which you can judge an author. If you are cautious and thorough in your approach, you can evaluate and critique an author's work as well as anyone. And once you have explored these thoughts, you will not only have a critic's insight into fiction, but you will enjoy it much more. See the following table for additional guidelines.

REVIEW THESE POINTS

*How to Evaluate Fiction
  1. Prepare for reading
  2. Meet the author
  3. Keep track of what you read
  4. Organize the information
  5. Ask questions before and after reading
  6. Learn ways to criticize an author's work

THE WORLDLY PHILOSOPHERS
by Robert Heilbroner
Chapter 3 — "The Wonderful World of Adam Smith"

BACKGROUND ON ENGLAND
Social Scene
Theology
Morality
Coal Mines

PERS. BIOG.
born 1723
Scotland
good student
U. of Glasgow
trav. Europe
died 1790

PERSONALITY TRAITS
friendly
nervous habits
well-known
absent-minded

MAJOR INFLUENCES ON HIM
Chas. Townshend (Ger.)
Dr. Quesnay (Fr.)
Ben Franklin (U.S.)

PUBLISHED WORKS
1759—Theory of Moral Sentiments
1776—Wealth of Nations
a revolutionary book
all encompassing

PHILOSOPHY

General	Law of Accumulation	Law of Population
"Laws of Market" Self-interest is imp. favors competition specialization whatever was cheaper, simpler, rational, expedient, unregulated.	favors accum. if re-channeled into society	as productivity increases/decreases population varies proportionately

Figure 9.
Sample Text Notes

These notes show the use of a variety of techniques useful in taking brief, well-organized, notes from a text book.

102

CHAPTER NINE

WRITE LIKE A WIZARD: THE SECRET OF TERM PAPERS

*"The most beautiful things in the world
are the most useless."*

Ruskin

For most students, writing a long paper is a terror. Few things are dreaded more, and for good reason. No one is really taught how to research and write a paper, so most go about it inefficiently. Yet when done properly, a research paper can not only be written quickly, but can be a lot of fun. This chapter shows you, step-by-step, how to produce the best paper you are capable of writing. The method outlined with make any paper well-structured, persuasive, and help you present your material for maximum results.

First, gather your sources, compile a bibliography, then preview and evaluate each. Next, you will prepare your notes in advance so you will have them all ready for the reading step. After reading you will double-check notes, write the paper from the notes, then proofread it and polish it.

Gather Sources. When you *gather sources* of information, try to locate the most recent ones written on your topic. In some fields, publications that are five years old may be outdated. Collect more sources than you think you will need because many may not be as useful as you hoped. Many short papers of five pages or less will require only two to five sources. A term paper of up to one hundred pages may require five to twenty sources to assure thorough coverage. While you investigate and gather sources, make a final decision about your topic, narrowing it to suit the length of your paper. Don't pick a topic too broad; World War II is a topic for a library of books, not a term paper. Make sure your topic is not too narrow; eighteenth-century kite flying in Southern France is obviously a bit limiting. You should spend a maximum of about two minutes per book or source, browsing through each to discover which are the best, and to categorize the books as core sources, borderline sources, or even to reject those which are too simplistic or redundant.

Compile your bibliography. List all sources you will use on a sheet of paper and number each of them. You will need to refer to that number later on in your notes. Also be sure to note all the related information about the sources including title, author, publisher, date and place of publication, and the volume and page numbers of magazines or periodicals.

Preview and evaluate sources. Dig into your sources, starting with the easiest first, and locate the best information. Look for information relevant to your topic but you don't need to read it at this point. Just note where it is. You might put light pencil marks in the margins to be erased later, or maybe just make a list on a separate piece of paper. Here your purpose is to become familiar with your topic, gaining basic background knowledge. This browsing time should take no more than five to ten minutes per source.

Before reading, design your notes. Plan your notes prior to reading. This allows you to categorize information as you come across it. Your notes will all fall under one of five areas which form the five basic sections of the paper. Keep a separate sheet for the introduction, background, facts, counter-arguments, and conclusion. No matter how long your paper ends up, you will use at least five pieces of paper. Keep a separate piece of paper for the introduction, background, facts, counter-arguments, and conclusion. Title each page and use as many pages as necessary for each category. After noting information, include the source number (you have already numbered them in your bibliography) and the page number that information came from. This will enable you to go back to that source later if necessary. List any important quotes at the bottom of your notes in a special section. Be sure to identify each quote by its number in the bibliography and page. No matter how long your paper ends up, you will have at least five pages of notes. You may have extra pages under a topic such as facts. Table 1 details information to be recorded for each category. Figure 11 illustrates the format for notetaking for a research paper.

Read for comprehension. Once you have gained background, prepared your notes, and isolated important information, reading will go faster. Again, start with the easiest source first, and read only the material that you have already noted as important. Don't read to memorize everything; that's why you are taking notes. After each important point, stop and add to one of your five topics. Every time you finish a section, you must decide what kind of information you read about. Was it background material, facts, or a good part for the conclusion of your paper?

Check and organize your notes. Check each topic heading and make sure you have enough information to write about. For example, if you do not have much data for a particular section of the paper, go back to your sources and find additional relevent material before you go any further. When you have completed compiling information for each section, organize the information into a logical sequence. Then you are ready to write.

Construct each section carefully. Table 8 described the main points to be covered in each section of the paper. A good introduction follows this sequence:

1. grab the reader's interest using an unusual or shocking quote or statement

THE WRITING WILL NOW BE EASY!

2. introduce the topic to the reader, explaining the width and depth of discussion
3. motivate the reader to want to read on by stressing the importance or relevance of your topic.

Background should include:

1. an interesting discussion of the history of your topic which enables the reader to understand your paper
2. the position or situation things are in today as they effect your topic
3. define the terminology you wish to use, especially if you will be using unusual definitions to common words.

The section which presents arguments is the bulk and power of your paper, and should:

1. state strongly and truthfully your viewpoint and all the facts, figures, data, and arguments which back up your thesis
2. use powerful, convincing language
3. present arguments from the weakest to the strongest, allowing the reader to become comfortable with your data without growing immediately defensive.

The section which discusses counter-arguments should:

1. state opposing viewpoints
2. point out the weaknesses in opposing viewpoints
3. refute by presenting evidence

For example, let us say that you were trying to convince the reader that a microwave oven is a good investment. But the reader may be thinking how costly they are to buy and operate. You should disarm his objections by reminding them the initial cost is easily offset by the savings in time and convenience. The operating costs are lower, not higher, because a microwave oven is used for shorter periods of time. Your rebuttal will actually reinforce your arguments by showing your awareness of opposing viewpoints.

The summary should:

1. rephrase the thesis as clearly as possible
2. review the most significant arguments in new words
3. conclude with a moving, dramatic synopsis

This is the reader's last impression, and your last opportunity to make clear your position. It's your last chance to convince the reader of the truth of your thesis. Always end on a positive note.

Because your notes are so complete and well-organized, each idea will flow into the next thought because you have already arranged them. Use a dictionary and thesaurus to clean up and flavor your writing. Write in simple, powerful sentences avoiding excessive wordiness. Use colorful examples whenever possible. To insure correctness of method and style, consult the MLA (Modern Language Association) style sheet.

Edit and proofread your final draft. After typing your paper, check it for mistakes. Edit for consistency of style, logical structure, correct usage and grammar, spelling, and accuracy of data. Put it down for a while, then look at it again. The time lapse will give you a fresh viewpoint and help reduce errors. Be sure to correct errors, as they will hurt your grade more than an erasure mark. Rewrite any sections that may need polish.

Review Table 10 for a compilation of the eight steps toward writing a research paper. If you follow these steps carefully, you should be ready for your professor. And you should be ready for an *A!*

REVIEW THESE POINTS

*Steps for Writing Papers
  1. Gather sources
  2. Preview and evaluate sources
  3. Compile bibliography
  4. Design your notes
  5. Read for comprehension
  6. Check and organize notes
  7. Construct each section
  8. Edit and proofread your final draft

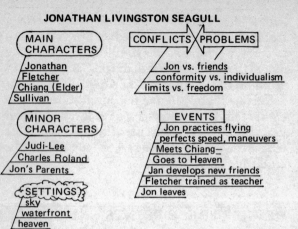

JONATHAN LIVINGSTON SEAGULL

MAIN CHARACTERS
Jonathan
Fletcher
Chiang (Elder)
Sullivan

CONFLICTS × PROBLEMS
Jon vs. friends
conformity vs. individualism
limits vs. freedom

MINOR CHARACTERS
Judi-Lee
Charles Roland
Jon's Parents

EVENTS
Jon practices flying
perfects speed, maneuvers
Meets Chiang—
Goes to Heaven
Jan develops new friends
Fletcher trained as teacher
Jon leaves

SETTINGS
sky
waterfront
heaven

Figure 10.
Possible Format for Organizing Fiction

110

HOW TO TAKE TESTS: SCORING WHAT YOU'RE WORTH

"The best students study what they don't know, not what they do know."

Jensen

PREPARING FOR TESTING

The first and most obvious preparation for taking tests is to study beforehand. But an effective study procedure which will help ensure success is one that is planned from the beginning of the course and carried on, step-by-step, throughout the school term.

1. First Few Weeks of Classes.

To ace your tests, start the first week of school. Find out about your instructor. What is his or her favorite topic or author? Is student creativity encouraged or is the class run by the rules? What kind of classwork is expected? Exactly what should your homework look like? Try to read ahead in your texts. Take notes before you go to class, it saves time and increases your understanding. As you read, ask questions of yourself or bring them to class. Add class lecture notes to your home text notes, always trying to consolidate and unify them.

2. Middle of Course.

Try to study a little every day. It's a lot more effective and less stressful than cramming. Ask questions when you don't understand course material. Don't put them off or you will forget about them. See your professor for extra help early in the term, not the day before a test. It will show a genuine interest on your part, and the extra contact will pay off at test time. Most importantly, be sure to introduce yourself, give your name twice, and make the most favorable impression you can. It's also helpful to ask your professor if he or she has any suggested reading material outside of assigned class texts. Even if you don't read that material, let your teacher know you're interested. The secret is to show some genuine interest in both your class subject and the professor. He or she is like anyone else and appreciates the personal touch.

Read as much background material as possible. The more you read about a topic, the greater your understanding, and the faster you will be able to read it. Gaining a wide background in a subject area will give you a big edge at test time. Another student may read the text and be able to recall most of it, but you will have the advantage even if you can recall only part of the additional reading you have done. You should also check your notes occasionally to make sure they are familiar and understandable.

3. The Last Week Before the Test.

Find out what kind of exam will be given and alter your studying accordingly. If an objective test is scheduled, use memory techniques and concentrate on details. For a subjective or essay exam, the best approach is to get a wide background in that subject, stressing ideas rather than details. Concentrate on knowing something about almost everything. Rework your notes into a new format, trying to see the material from new angles. Review sessions are helpful, but only get together with others if they are good students. Otherwise, you will be really "soaked" for information, and learn nothing yourself. A *C* student usually doesn't enlighten an honor student, so study with the best students you can.

4. Last Few Days Before the Test.

At this point, start identifying what you don't know. Many students review by going over material they already know well. Often, parts they don't know are ignored, making their study process ineffective. Don't pat yourself on the back for what you do know, find out what you don't know. Remember this secret on how to study for tests: Turn to the index of your textbook and start with the first entry. Ask yourself if you understand that term, and continue until you come across an unfamiliar term. Look it up in the text, read about it, then take notes on it so you won't forget again. This system allows you to check yourself on every term, idea, person, and detail in the entire textbook. If your test is only on chapters seven and eight, just turn to the table of contents and find out which pages those chapters cover. Suppose those chapters include pages 77 through 102. Turn to the index again, and start at the beginning again. But this time look down the right side, noting only the terms which are on pages 77 through 102. That way you will only study the chapters you will be tested on.

Turn to the end of your text chapters and review a summary or listing of author's questions.

This can be helpful in directing your study efforts. At many colleges and universities, tests used during previous terms are kept on file in the library. These can be a gold mine because many professors don't rewrite a test each term. Often the tests used may just be scrambled questions from old tests. The prepared student has an easy *A*.

Many students find the use of homemade flash cards ideal, because they are portable and sometimes even fun. You might put a possible test question on one side and the answer on the other. Make notes on any data you seem to forget easily. Certain things seem very easy to remember and others seem easy to forget. But remember, if you forget it once, you will forget it again unless you write it down.

A positive attitude is crucial the few days prior to an exam. The upcoming test is not an execution; it is just a chance to show what you have learned. Your instructors want you to get good grades because it reflects on their teaching success. Most instructors feel badly when students do poorly because that mirrors their failure to communicate important concepts. Look at the exam as a challenge and an opportunity to show what you have learned. Admit to yourself that you probably won't know every question; that way, you won't get discouraged when you see a test question you can't answer. Tests are necessary in most subjects. They're about the only way the professor knows you know the material.

5. Hours Before the Exam.

You have already run the hardest part of the race. If you have kept up during the term, you have already passed the exam; now it is the difference between an *A* and a *B*. Others may have exam fever, but you can relax a bit. Get a full night's sleep and be sure to get some exercise the day of the exam. That encourages better blood circulation, hence a better supply of oxygen to your brain during exam time. You will be able to think more clearly. It is best to exercise in moderation so that you are invigorated rather than exhausted. A brisk walk before the test is a good way to get exercise. Eat good foods, but eat lightly or not at all within an hour of your test. If you do, your body's energy and blood supply will be drawn towards your stomach for digestion instead of towards your brain where it is needed during test time.

Be sure to review all notes and texts. Browse through each chapter making certain to expose your mind to as much information as possible. If you have kept up, all will be a review and cramming won't be necessary. Your confidence and calm mental attitude will encourage recall at test time. A review on the night before the test should only take two to three hours. On the day of the exam arrive five to ten minutes early to your class. The best way to relax is to prepare mentally. Get the seat you want in class and practice recalling.

6. Exam Time.

Now you can cash in your efforts. First, read the entire exam thoroughly. By seeing questions in advance, you will give your subconscious mind time to come up with answers. Second, allot your time wisely. Note which questions are given the most point value and which are most difficult. Don't pick up your pen for a few minutes. Stop to think about your attack plan. Be relaxed and calm while you plan your approach. A good test-taker doesn't fight tests; the secret is to relax.

Interpret and rephrase questions several ways to be sure you understand them. Then, start with the easiest problems first, and work quickly and neatly. Structure and organize before you answer because neatness does count, regardless of what an instructor will say. Be sure to keep in mind the test directions as you answer. Don't over-read questions by assuming they are more complex than at first glance. Read them for what you believe is the intent of the question. Notice critical or key words in each question such as "show", "contrast", "define", and other similar direc-

DON'T OVERWORRY!

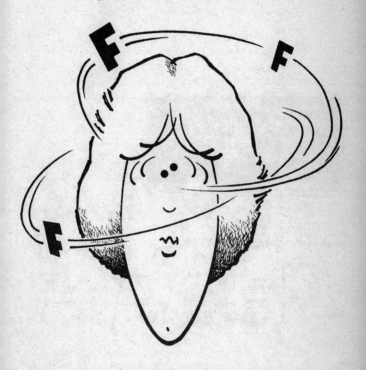

PREPARATION MEANS <u>CONFIDENCE</u>!

tions. Try to answer every question unless you have absolutely no idea of the answer; wrong answers are often subtracted from right ones.

TAKING OBJECTIVE TESTS

Objective tests are those which include questions in a true-false, multiple-choice, matching, or fill-in format. Usually the answer is provided but the student must decide among several possibilities.

1. True-False Questions.

True-false questions are the easiest test questions for the obvious reason that you have at least a fifty-fifty chance of getting the right answer. First, be sure you have read the question correctly. Look for words such as *always* or *never*, these words often indicate a false answer. Words such as often, usually, rarely, or sometimes can indicate a true answer. Decide if the statement is totally true before you mark it true. Answer what the tester intended, not what you read into the question. For example, the statement, "General Motors produces compact cars," is true. If the question had read, "General Motors *alone* produces compact cars," then it would be false. On true-false questions, stick with your first impression. Studies have shown over and over that your first impression is usually right so be slow to change your answer, if at all. Remember a statement is more likely to be true if it is a fairly long statement; it takes more qualifiers to make a true statement than a false one.

2. Multiple-Choice Questions.

An important rule to remember when answering multiple-choice questions is to read the answers first. This way, you'll view each answer separately and equally, without "jumping" on the first and easiest one. Look for an answer which not only seems right on its own, but completes the question smoothly. If the question asks why something occurs, then your answer must be a cause. Try to eliminate any obviously poor answers. Suspect as a possible right answer phrases such as "all of the above," "none of the above," or "two of the above." Check the wording of questions to notice qualifying phrases such as "all of the following are true *except*..." or "which two of the below are *not*..." Statistically, the least likely correct answer on a multiple-choice question is the first choice. When in doubt, pick the longer of two answers. But, just as in true-false sections, always put something down. Even an educated guess is better than leaving the question blank and getting it wrong for sure.

3. Sentence Completion or fill-in Questions.

These generally ask for an exact word from memory. They don't allow for much error, so make sure your answer is a logical part of the sentence as a whole. Use the length and number of blanks given as a hint. Make sure the grammar is consistent. When in doubt, guess. Even if it's a generalized guess, you may get partial credit. If you are unsure of two possibilities, include both and hope for half credit.

TAKING ESSAY TESTS

When answering questions on an essay test, begin by making outline on a piece of scratch paper. Assemble and organize the main points. Check the wording of the question to make sure you are interpreting the question correctly. For example, if the question asks you to compare and contrast, do not give a description or a discussion. Begin your essay by using the same words in your answer that are in the question. Keep your answer to the point. Always write something in answer to a question, even if you don't have much to say. Think and write by using this format:

1. Introduction—Introduce your topic.
2. Background—Give historical or Philosophical background data to orient the reader to the topic.
3. Thesis and Arguments—State the main points, including causes and effects, methods used, dates, places, results.
4. Conclusion—Include the significance of each event and finish up with a summary.

When totally stumped for an answer on an essay, think about book titles, famous names, places, dates, wars, economics, and politics. Usually something will trigger some ideas. If you know nothing about the essay question, invent your own question on the subject and answer it. You'll usually get at least partial credit. That's better than nothing.

THE AFTERMATH

When you complete a test, be sure to re-read all your answers. Check the wording of the questions again. Eliminate careless errors, and you can save a lot of disappointment later. This is the time when you can cash in on your brief encounters with your professor. Write your name in large, visible letters. If you have made a positive impression on your professor from personal contact, it will pay off now. Sometimes just a good impression can give you the higher grade in a borderline situation. Take as much time as you need. When you think you have finished the test, turn it upside down on your desk. Think about it for a few minutes, giving your mind some time to relax and come up with some answers. If you still agree with what you have written, then turn it in. But sometimes those few moments spent just thinking about the questions will bring back the answer that gives the *A*.

Once your corrected test is returned, look it over. Check your errors and find out not what they were, but what kind of errors they were. Was it from answering questions too quickly, poor organization, a missed assignment, or incorrect notes? Understand why you made errors and avoid the problem on the next test.

REVIEW THESE POINTS

*Prepare for Tests
1. First few weeks of classes
2. Mid-course
3. The last week before the test
4. Last few days before the test
5. Hours before the exam
6. Exam time

*Take Objective Tests
  1. True-false
  2. Multiple choice
  3. Sentence completion or fill-in
*Take Essay Tests
  1. Outline
  2. Assemble and organize
  3. Write your introduction, background, thesis, and conclusion
  4. Re-read

1) Use at least five sheets of paper.

2) Title each one—introduction, background, facts, counter-arguments, and conclusions.

3) Use as many pages as necessary for each category, but title every page.

4) After each bit of information put in the source number (you have already numbered them in your bibliography) and the page number. This enables you to go back to that source later if necessary.

5) Put quotes at the bottom of notes in a special section. Be sure to put identifying numbers after each quote.

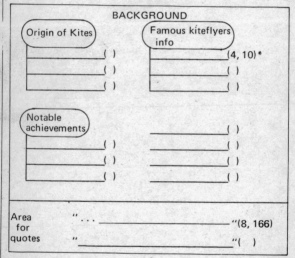

*Parentheses indicate the source number and book number.

Figure 11.
Format for Research Notes

122

CHAPTER ELEVEN

THE SECRET

"The worst thing one can do is not to try, to be aware of what one wants and not give into it, to spend years in silent hurt wondering if something could have materialized—and never knowing."
                    David S. Viscott

Throughout the book I've talked about the importance of building successful habits. I've given you many ways to help better yourself in school. As you've been able to tell, much of what is normally considered success in school can be achieved by positive thinking. In almost every chapter, you've seen how a positive approach can help you improve.

Yet, as vital as this is, there is more. Your mind is capable of much more, as it is your most powerful possession. Utilize what you've learned so far, then add the secret I'm about to give you and every problem can become an opportunity, every setback a shortcut, and every question an answer. The secret in this chapter will provide you with the last part of the formula for total success.

Like all real success formulas, the secret is simple. So far we have explored the conscious ways one can become successful. But perhaps you have never given thought to the other 88% of your mind, the subconscious.

One cannot overemphasize how fully it controls your life. Your subconscious mind functions automatically and ceaselessly twenty-four hours a day. It is an unlimited and perfect computer. It's a storehouse of forgotten dreams, nightmares, skills, and suggestions. And since it has the accumulations of a lifetime, much of its stored information is out of date. So, although your subconscious has the capacity of a $10 billion supercomputer, like any computer, it is only as good as the programmer. Years ago, improper programming created bad habits that are not broken by the willpower of the conscious mind. To be a dynamic total success, you must reprogram the subconscious mind. Therein lies the secret!

The most direct and simple way to reprogram the subconscious mind is through hypnosis. Under hypnosis the door to your subconscious is wide open. Your master inner computer will accept suggestions easily and without question. You may have seen the power of these hypnotic suggestions in a stage show. A timid, shy individual can be told that he is a great orator and he will proceed to give an eloquent talk to an amazed audience.

You may have some negative feelings about using hypnosis because of myths perpetuated by movies, television, stories, or stage shows. Yet every one of us passes through a brief hypnotic stage several times a day. This stage occurs just before falling asleep at night, upon awaking in the morning, and during times of extreme relaxation. During these moments of near sleep your normally argumentative conscious mind is not being used and suggestions are easily implanted in the subconscious mind. Why not use this natural state of mind to give positive suggestions of successful school habits directly to the subconscious, where they would be certain to take effect? After all, hypnosis merely implies a heightened state of suggestibility and there is nothing difficult or dangerous involved. It is totally safe and you are in full control at all times.

Since it's often inconvenient to have others hypnotize you, self-hypnosis is the answer. In self-hypnosis, you'll discover a totally self-contained and self-controlled relaxed state of mind. You'll have full control over each suggestion. The suggestions you give yourself will go directly to your subconscious and allow you to reach your goals quickly and effortlessly. Not just any kind of suggestion will help so let's define the proper kinds.

Suggestions, or affirmations as they are often called, have been used for thousands of years. An affirmation is a reinforcement tool used to affect our thoughts or actions in order to reach a goal. Affirmations can be written down, spoken, or visual. In order for affirmations to be effective, they should be positive, short, and in the present tense. For example, you would say "I read rapidly and effortlessly," not "I no longer read slowly."

You might ask "How can I say I'm a fast reader when I'm not? Aren't I lying?" No, you are not lying. You are using your power of choice to reprogram your subconscious. After all, it does not know the difference between true or false. It will accept, without questioning anything you program into it. Therefore, if you repeatedly state "I *am* a rapid reader," you'll find your subconscious mind accepting that affirmation and soon you'll be one.

Affirmations can become doubly effective when coupled with another tool, visualizations. As you program your subconscious with each positive suggestion, visualize yourself having accomplished it. See yourself achieving that suggestion and reaching the goal you intended. Feel the excitement and joy of success. This will speed you on your way to realization of your goals.

Speaking of goals, you may already have a good idea of the goals you'd like to achieve while you're in school. If not, some of the more common ones are listed below and the corresponding affirmations you can use to help you reach those goals.

GOAL: IMPROVED STUDY SKILLS

Suggested affirmations: I enjoy studying. I look forward to studying every day. I have plenty of time to study and find every subject interesting. I am enthusiastic and excited about studying. I always browse through textbooks before reading them. I observe the style, organization, and vocabulary. I prepare each section before reading. I gather main ideas quickly and easily. I read my texts with excellent comprehension. I review each chapter quickly and thoroughly. My notes are superb.

GOAL: BETTER READING SKILLS

Suggested affirmations: I love to read and find plenty of time for reading. I read quickly and effortlessly. I read in large word groups, absorbing difficult material without hesitation. My comprehension is perfect, as is my retention.

GOAL: IMPROVED NOTETAKING

Suggested affirmations: I enjoy taking notes and find them easy to do well. My notes represent the material clearly and creatively. I use my own shorthand and vary the size and shape of headings. I know the basic formats of most subjects and use it when designing my notes.

GOAL: IMPROVED MEMORY

Suggested affirmations: My memory is perfect and I enjoy remembering information. I retain my material with ease and completeness. My memory is improving and I am more aware each day. Whatever information I need comes to me instantly and easily through perfect recall.

GOAL: INCREASING VOCABULARY

Suggested affirmations: I have an ever-increasing vocabulary and enjoy learning new words. I read new and unusual materials thus adding new words daily. I have flash cards and practice them daily. I associate with those who have an excellent vocabulary to learn new words. I use the dictionary to increase my vocabulary. I notice how new words are spelled and check for the root words. I enjoy an excellent vocabulary and use it daily.

GOAL: BETTER TEST-TAKING

Suggested affirmations: I look forward to taking tests and enjoy the opportunity to show what I know. I prepare myself thoroughly for each test. I review all class lecture notes, textbook notes and related data. I easily memorize all pertinent information. I am confident and relaxed at exam time. I first preview the test, then plan my strategy. I move quickly and effortlessly through the exam. Correct answers come to mind instantly. My answers are clear and true. I am a successful test-taker.

GOAL: CONCENTRATION

Suggested affirmations: I am able to concentrate with ease. I block out distractions quickly and automatically. I focus my mind on the task at hand and complete it accurately. Other noises that I hear are normal every day sounds which flow with my thinking and increase my concentration.

GOAL: BETTER HEALTH

Suggested affirmations: I enjoy perfect health. I am energetic, enthusiastic and outgoing. I enjoy small portions of health-giving wholesome foods. I experience an abundance of energy, vibrance, and youth. My body functions perfectly. I am alert, healthy and strong. I keep my body in perfect condition and exercise daily. I enjoy exercising and my body is becoming firmer, stronger, and full of vitality. I think only thoughts of health, energy, and life.

GOAL: LIKING SCHOOL

Suggested affirmations: I enjoy my classes and look forward to attending them daily. I thirst for knowledge. I satisfy my need for knowledge by attending all my classes and consulting my instructor. I find school challenging, rewarding, and positive. I meet interesting people at school and form satisfying relationships. I have an intense desire to become a success and school is the key for me.

GOAL: THINKING POSITIVE OF OTHERS

Suggested affirmations: I enjoy positive thoughts. I look for the good in others. I practice the Golden Rule, knowing that a smile is powerful. I feel comfortable with others and find compliments easy to give. I allow others to be who they are, and give them understanding and warmth.

GOAL: INCREASED CONFIDENCE

Suggested affirmations: I am the most important person in my world. I am successful. I am an intelligent free-willed being with the power to choose. I am talented, capable, and honest. I am warm, sincere, worthy, and creative. I like myself. I have a tremendous and unlimited potential. I love myself and appreciate my talents and abilities. I am unique and rare. I am valuable and rich in thought. I am an expression of love, happiness, and confidence. I believe in myself and my future. I am calm, relaxed and confident in any situation I choose. I control my destiny. I am free.

From the suggestions above, pick the affirmations which will help you reach the goals you desire. Many students find that writing affirmations down on 3-x-5-inch cards helps to clarify exactly what is wanted and is a convenient way to reinforce the goals. Anytime you have some free moments, you can read through your affirmations for reinforcement. By the way, there is no limit to the number of affirmations you may use. Certainly, you'd want several affirmations per card, and to use at least 30 cards.

Are you ready to put it all together? Let's first be aware hypnosis is a perfectly natural state of mind. It occurs between sleep and waking consciousness. During this relaxed state you will feel peaceful, serene and passive. You will hear normal outside noises but they will not disturb you. You will be able to think clearly but often your mind will wander.

Upon awakening from his or her first hypnotic experience, a student will often say "I didn't feel a thing." They will often wonder if they were even hypnotized. But each time self-hypnosis is used, you'll find yourself going into relaxation deeper and more quickly. Therefore, do not concern yourself with degree of depth. The suggestions will reach your subconscious and repetition is the key.

There are many symptoms of hypnosis but initially do not concern yourself with the technical nature of them. Simply allow your-self to relax and you may experience several of the symptoms below indicating you are in a hypnotic stage:

1. physical relaxation
2. head and hands fall to side
3. heaviness of limbs
4. deep and rhythmic breathing
5. wanting to swallow
6. tingling sensation in fingers and toes
7. hand moves slowly to scratch an itch
8. sounds fade in and out
9. drowsiness and motionless
10. time passes quickly

Here are simple steps for you to induce self-hypnosis. There are other techniques, but this particular method is extremely easy, yet effective.

DIRECTIONS FOR SELF-HYPNOSIS

1. Collect your affirmations (self-improvement suggestions on 3-x-5-inch cards).
2. Relax in a comfortable chair.
3. Read your affirmations.
4. Close your eyes and relax.
5. Inhale deeply, hold the first breath to the count of four, then exhale slowly.
6. Inhale deeply, hold your breath to count of six, then exhale slowly.
7. Inhale deeply, hold your breath to count of eight, then exhale slowly.

8. Starting with the muscles in your neck, relax each of your major muscles. Do your shoulders, arms, hands. Continue down as you relax your stomach, thighs and legs. Relax every muscle in your body and allow it to remain loose and limp.

9. Visualize the accomplishment of your affirmations. Imagine your successes in great detail. See the goal attained and actually feel the excitement.

10. Slowly awaken yourself by counting from one to five. During this brief re-entry to your conscious mind, give yourself suggestions of happiness, alertness and vitality.

You may choose to remain in a hypnotic stage for as little as five minutes or as long as thirty minutes. The length is not as important as is the frequency. Use your self-hypnosis often because the more often you gain access to your subconscious, the faster you'll reach your goals.

Practice your hypnosis at least once per day although three times per day would be more helpful. Here are some good times to practice it: Upon awakening in the morning, during a break, on a picnic in a park, while sunning yourself outside, during a boring TV show, and before you get out of your car.

Sometimes students become overwhelmed at this point because it all seems so complicated. But the procedure is incredibly simple and rewarding. You can change old bad habits without effort or sacrifice. Each time you read your affirmations something positive happens.

You are making a definite step towards your goal because every affirmation will register.

Do not become discouraged if the results are not immediate. As long as you continue to use your self-hypnosis, you are breaking down old objections and resistance. The positive suggestions will then become stronger than the old habits and you will begin acting successfully. It will be comfortable and natural.

You may be amazed to realize that you once objected to your new goals and now it seems so normal. You will have established a new habit pattern, improved your confidence, self-image, and of course, your school habits. More importantly, you'll affirm, and will be forever aware, that you are in control of your life. Your life will happen by your design and not by chance. Therefore, if you design it well, through effective affirmations, you can have the life you want.

Now that you have learned about affirmations, you can see the purpose of the Daily Scroll at the front of this book. In fact, you may want to include it in your daily self-hypnosis. The use of the Daily Scroll can help make your steps to self-hypnosis even easier. Let's review the steps:

1. Decide on your goals.
2. Write down affirmations which will help you reach your goals on 3-x-5-inch cards.
3. Repeat several times a day.

Simple enough isn't it? Yes, it is a small price to pay for the benefits of being successful. Yet, this is the challenge for everyone, the challenge of change. Change is not easy sometimes, but in this case it *is* easy. And it's exciting. The feeling of success you'll acquire would be worth a lifetime of savings. There's nothing like it. For true success is not to be measured in the material world, it is a feeling. It's a gut-level feeling of pride, accomplishment, contentment, abundance, and joy. Because if you have that feeling, the feeling self-hypnosis and positive thinking can give to you, then you'll be a success in anything. Not just school, but in relationships, athletics, business, and life.

My goal in this book was to give you three things. I want you to realize that you *can* become a total success in school. You have all the ability and talent in the world. Whatever you wish in life can be yours if you'll only realize it and accept it.

Secondly, I wanted to *motivate* you to achieve what you know you can. Everyone is motivated by different things and I hope you've found the right motivation for you to begin being successful. Reading this book shows you've already motivated yourself well.

Lastly, I wanted to give you the *tools* to achieve all the success which is rightfully yours. You've been given many valuable tools in this book: the knowledge of an excellent study procedure, how to read better, how to take more effective notes, how to improve your vocabulary, how to remember better, techniques for evaluating fiction, how to write papers, and secrets to taking tests. You've learned how to program a better future through self-hypnosis and what an important tool that is! Now that you've finished this book, put what you've learned to use. You know you deserve success, so go for it!

BASIC SPELLING RULES

MID-WORD SPELLING

Rule: 1) Use *ie* when the sound is ee except after c.

EXAMPLES: rel*ie*f

                   ach*ie*ve

                   gr*ie*f

EXCEPTIONS: n*ei*ther

                   w*ei*rd

                   l*ei*sure

      2) Use *ei* when the sound is not ee.

EXAMPLES: r*ei*gn

                   *ei*ght

                   w*ei*gh

EXCEPTIONS: fr*ie*nd

                   misch*ie*f

PLURALS

Definition: A plural form of a word is used to increase quantity:

Rule: 1) With most nouns, simply add the letter *s*.

EXAMPLES: teachers
               pencils
               books

2) In some nouns, the plural is formed with an *es*.

EXAMPLES: boxes
               matches
               dishes

3) If the noun ends with a *y* which is preceeded by a consonant, change *y* to *i* and add *es*.

EXAMPLES: flies
               daisies
               countries

4) The plural of nouns ending in a *y* proceeded by a vowel is formed by adding an *s*

EXAMPLES: valleys
               freeways
               plays

5) In some nouns ending in *f* or *fe* change the *f* to *v* and add *es*.

EXAMPLES: shelves
               knives
               wolves

6) The plural of nouns ending in *o* preceeded by a consonant is formed by adding *es*.

EXAMPLES: tomatoes
               dominoes
               torpedoes

7) For nouns which refer to music ending in *o,* and *s*.

EXAMPLES: radios
               stereos
               pianos

8) The plural of some irregular nouns are formed by changing the vowels to *e*'s.

EXAMPLES: tooth — t*ee*th
woman — wom*en*
goose — g*ee*se

9) The plural of word phrases is formed by making only the key word plural.

EXAMPLES: maid*s* of honor
editor*s* in chief
m*en* of war

10) The plural of numbers, letters, and signs is formed by adding an apostrophe and *s*.

EXAMPLES: 1800*'s*
abc*'s*
t*'s*

SUFFIXES

Definition: A suffix is a letter or group of letters added to the end of a word to change its meaning.

Rule: 1) The spelling of the base word remains the same *if* the suffix begins with a consonant.

EXAMPLES: arrange*ment*
casual*ly*
sharp*ness*
peace*ful*

2) Drop the final *e* in the base word if it is silent and the suffix begins with a vowel.

139

EXAMPLES: creat*ing*
     surpris*ed*
EXCEPTIONS: notic*eable*
     outrag*eous*
  3) In one syllable words ending in a single consonant and preceded by a single vowel, double the consonant.
EXAMPLES: dropp*ed*
     fall*en*
     swimm*ing*

PREFIXES

Definition: A prefix is a letter or group of letters added to the beginning of a word to change its meaning.

Rule: 1) When adding prefixes, the spelling of the original word remains the same.

EXAMPLES: il + logical = illogical
     in + active = inactive
     un + easy = uneasy
     dis + order = disorder
     im + possible = impossible
     mis + take = mistake
     re + do = redo
     over + eat = overeat
     under + fed = underfed

  2) When adding *so* or *self*, use a hyphen to separate the words.

EXAMPLES: so-called
     self-hypnosis
     self-made

BIBLIOGRAPHY

Adler, Mortimer. *How to Read a Book*. New York: Simon and Schuster, 1940.

Aiken, Daymond. *You Can Learn to Study*. New York: Holt, Rinehart, and Winston, 1953.

Armstrong, William. *Study is Hard Work*. New York: Harper & Row, 1967.

Bamman, Henry, and Brammer Lawrence. *How to Study Successfully*. Palo Alto, California: Pacific Books, 1969.

Borger, and Seaborne. *The Psychology of Learning*. Baltimore: Penguin Books, 1966.

Branden, Nathaniel. *The Psychology of Self-Esteem*. New York: Bantom, 1969.

Brothers, Joyce, *Ten Days to a Successful Memory*. New Jersey: Prentice-Hall, 1957.

Brown, James. *Efficient Reading*. Lexington: D. C. Heath & Co., 1967.

Brownstein, Samuel, and Weiner Mitchel. *How to Prepare for the PSAT-NMSQT*. Woodbury, New York: Barron Publishing Co., 1976.

Campbell, David. *If You Don't Know Where You're Going, You'll Probably End Up Somewhere Else*. Niles, Illinois: Argus Communications, 1974.

Chapman, Elwood. *So You're a College Freshman*. Chicago: Science Research Associates, 1967.

Crawford, Claude. *Studying the Major Subjects*. Los Angeles: C.C. Crawford, 1930.

Crawford, Claude. *The Technique of Study*. New York: Houghton-Mifflin, 1928.

Crawley, S.L. *Studying Efficiently*. New York: Prentice-Hall, 1936.

Dimnet, Ernest. *The Art of Thinking*. New York: Fawcett, 1928.

Dudley, Geoffrey. *Increase Your Learning Power*. Hollywood: Wilshire, 1975.

Duker, R. *The Truth About Your Child's Reading*. New York: Crown Publishers, Inc., 1956.

Dunn-Rankin, Peter. "Visual Characteristics of Words.' *Scientific American* 238:128, 1978.

Elliot, Harry. *The Effective Student*. New York: Harper & Row, 1966.

Ellis, Albert. *A New Guide to Rational Living*. Hollywood: Wilshire, 1977.

Flesch, Rudolph. *How You Can Be a Better Student*. New York: Sterling Publishing Co., 1957.

Fralick, Marsha. *Decisions Make It Happen*. La Mesa, California: Grossmont Union High Press, 1977.

Froe, Otis. *How To Become a Successful Student*. New York: Arco Publishing Co., 1959.

Garfield, Pat. *Creative Dreaming*. New York: Ballantine, 1974.

Glasser, William. *Schools Without Failure*. New York: Harper & Row, 1969.

Harris, Albert. *How to Increase Reading Ability*. New York: Longmans, Green, and Co., 1956.

Harrison, Allan. *How To Teach Children Twice As Much*. New York: Arlington House, 1973.

Hill, Napoleon. *Think and Grow Rich.* New York: Fawcett, 1937.

Hunter, Ian. *Memory.* London: Cox & Wyman, 1957.

Kidd, J.R. *How Adults Learn.* New York: Association Press, 1959.

Kranyik, Robert. *How to Teach Study Skills.* New Jersey: Teachers Practical Press, 1963.

Laird, Donald and Eleanor. *Techniques for Efficient Remembering.* New York: McGraw-Hill, 1968.

Lakein, Alan. *How To Get Control Of Your Time and Your Life.* New York: Signet, 1974.

Leedy, Paul. *Improve Your Reading.* New York: McGraw-Hill, 1956.

Lewis, Norman. *How to Read Better and Faster.* New York: John Wiley & Sons, 1969.

Lindgren, H. *The Psychology of College Success.* New York: John Wiley & Sons, 1969.

Lucas, Jerry, and Lorayne, Harry. *The Memory Book.* New York: McMillan, 1974.

Mace, C. *The Psychology of Study.* Gretna, Louisiana: Pelican, 1963.

Maddox, H. *How to Study.* New York: Fawcett-Crest, 1966.

Maltz, Maxwell. *Psycho-Cybernetics.* Hollywood: Wilshire Book Co., 1960.

Mandino, Og. *The Greatest Miracle in the World.* New York: Bantam, 1975.

Mandino, Og. *The Greatest Salesman in the World.* New York: Bantam, 1968.

Mayer, Dennis. *X-Rated Guide to Learning.* Fullerton, California: CPGA, 1978.

Millman, Jason. *How to Take Tests.* New York: McGraw-Hill 1969.

Morgan, Clifford. *How to Study.* New York: McGraw-Hill, 1969.

Orchard, N. *Study Successfully*. New York: McGraw-Hill, 1953.

Ornstein, Robert. *Psychology of Consciousness*. San Francisco: Penguin, 1974.

Ornstein, Robert. *The Mind Field*. New York: Pocket Books, 1976.

Pauk, Walter. *How to Study in College*. New York: Houghton-Mifflin, 1962.

Pettit, Lincoln. *How to Study and Take Exams*. New York: J. Rider, 1960.

Pitkin, Walter. *The Art of Rapid Reading*. New York: McGraw-Hill, 1929.

Preston, Ralph. *How to Study*. Chicago: Science Research Associates, 1956.

Robinson, Frank. *Effective Study*. New York: Harper & Row, 1946.

Ross, John. "Resources of Binocular Perception." *Scientific American* March 1976:80.

Rusk, Thomas. *Treat Your Ego in 4 Hours*. New York: Peter Wyden Publisher, 1974.

Schwartz, E. Samuel. *How to Double Your Child's Grades in School*. New York: Executive Research Institute, 1964.

Shefter, Harry, *Faster Reading Self-taught*. New York: Washington Square Press, 1958.

Sill, Sterling, *How You Can Personally Profit From the Laws of Success*. Salt Lake City, Utah, NIFP (National Institute of Financial Planning), 1978.

Smith, Samuel. *Best Methods of Study*. New York: Barnes & Noble, 1968.

Staton, Thomas. *How to Study*. Nashville: McQuiddy, 1954.

Strang, Ruth. *Helping Your Child Improve His Reading*. New York: E.P. Dutton, 1962.

Tussing, Lyle. *Study and Succeed*. New York: John Wiley & Sons, 1962.

Weinland, James. *How to Improve Your Memory*. New York: Barnes & Noble, 1957.

Witty, Paul. *How to Become a Better Reader*. Chicago: Science Research Associates.

Wood, Evelyn. *Reading Skills*. New York: Holt, Rinehart, & Winston, 1958.

Wrightstone, Wayne. *How to Be a Better Student*. New York: Science Research Associates, 1956.

TABLES

Table 1	Symbols for Use in Notetaking
SYMBOL	EXPLANATION
$>$	greater than, more than
$<$	less than
$=$	the same, equals
$\neq$	not the same, different
$\times$	times, cross, trans
$\rightarrow$	towards, going
$\leftarrow$	from
$\therefore$	therefore, because
∞	infinity, a great deal
(+)	positive, good
(−)	negative, against
$\overline{c}$, w/	with
w/o	without
$\downarrow$	down, under, decreasing
$\uparrow$	above, up, increasing
\$	dollars, money
Q	question
A	answer

Table 2. **Geometric Key for Use in Notetaking**

GEOMETRIC SYMBOL	EXPLANATION
☐	Main Ideas: Inserted in square or √ Marked with check
√ √	Important Concepts or Facts to Remember: Marked with two checks
⬭	Names of People: Circled
▭	Minor Ideas or Details: Inserted in rectangle
△	Reasons, Why, How: Inserted in triangle
⟶ LETTER SIZE	Relationships or Connecting Ideas: Indicated by arrows and letter size to show subordinate ideas

Table 3. Basic Subject Formats

SUBJECT AREA	FORMAT AND STRUCTURE
Social Sciences	
Law	Issues and principles
Political Science	Background information
Sociology	Problems, conflicts
Psychology	Reasoning, procedure
Psychology	Decisions, results
History	Conclusions, alternatives
Exact Sciences	
Math	Background, idea
Biology	description
Physics	Laws, theorems, axioms
Chemistry	Supportive examples, approach
	New problems to solve
	Solutions, other applications
Literature	
Novels	Background on author,
Plays	topic
Poetry	Characters
	Problems, issues defined
	Events, complications
	Crises, problem solved

Table 4. Lecture Notetaking Responsibilities

Responsibility	Objective	Procedure
Listen	Anticipate your purpose	Decide if you need to remember everything in the lecture or only main ideas.
		Determine what material you will be responsible for on a test.
		Determine if the lecture is a complement to your reading assignment or new material.
	Spend most of your time listening, not taking notes.	Listen to understand
		Listen for entire ideas.
		Summarize ideas.
		Determine the main points.
		Decide how the main points are being made.
	Think and concentrate as you listen.	Note examples given.
		Decide if you agree with the main points.
		Determine if your previous knowledge allows you to interpret the information differently than the presentation.
		Try to recall the lecture so that you could present the information covered to someone else.
Take Notes	Be brief.	Write main ideas first. Write details if time allows.
	Use key words.	Write words which will allow recall of additional information presented.
	Use symbols	Take notes using symbols, underlining, pictures, cartoons, and arrows
	Have extra supplies	Carry spare pens, pencils, and paper.
	Review and reorganize	Go over notes, rewrite or add extra information while they are fresh in your mind.

Table 5. Forming Associations Between Random Words

Item	Think of	Then associate...
table	an enormous table, or a particular table, such as your kitchen table	
dance	imagine a dance	imagine the table dancing, up on two legs
duck	an enormous, overstuffed, 6 foot duck, white with orange feet and bill	imagine the duck doing this wild dance
walnuts	millions of walnuts falling out of the sky	imagine the walnuts between the toes
toes	your own toes	imagine huge walnuts between your toes
mirror	very small mirrors the size of a stamp	picture mirrors on the toes instead of toenails
bear	picture a huge brown bear, with your clothes on	imagine the bear seeing himself in the mirror
canoe	picture a dugout canoe	picture the bear paddling around in a canoe
necklace	an enormous, long one	imagine huge canoes around an enormous necklace
fire	crackling and extra hot	imagine the necklace so hot it's on fire— remove it!

Table 6. Ten Common Root Words

Root	Meaning	Usage
con-	with, for	conjugal, confident, contemporary
rad-	moving away from	radio, radiate, radial
bi- (also tri; quad, etc.)	two, dual	bicycle, bipartisan, bicentennial
-logy	word	apology, catalogue, dialogue
chron-	time	chronology, chronicle, chronometer
gen-	people	gentile, genius, general
auto-	self	automatic, autograph, autonomy, author
trans-	across	transfer, transmit, transportation
graph-	write	multigraph, graffiti, graph, phonograph
sub-	below	submerge, submit, submarine

Table 7. Common Errors in Spelling and Usage

Word	Meaning	Usage
quite quiet	very without noise	The soup was **quite** hot. The room was **quiet**.
then than	shows time compares	**Then** he went home. He is taller **than** I am.
to	gives direction or infinitive form of verb	Give it **to** me. I like **to** run.
two	a number	I have read **two** books today.
too	also, or excess	I want to go **too**. I am **too** tired.
weather whether	relating to climate involves decision	We had nice **weather** today. I don't know **whether** it's right.
accept except	to receive to exclude	Will he **accept** the gift? Everyone laughed **except** Bob.
lose loose	opposite of to find not tight	I did not **lose** it. The belt was **loose**.
already all ready	shows time prepared	It's **already** dinner time. She was **all ready**.
its it's	shows possession means it is	The dog wagged **its** tail. **It's** going to be hot.
they're	means they are	**They're** not at home.
there	usually shows location or opens a sentence	Sit over **there**.
their	shows possession	**Their** house.
used to	supposed to	I **used to** visit often
a lot	means a great deal (a vague expression)	That's **a lot** of fun.
take for instance or take for example	do not use when you really mean "for example	WRONG: My father is an awful driver. **Like** last week . . . RIGHT: My father is an awful driver. **For example**, last week . . .

Word	Meaning	Usage
you	do not use unless you actually mean the reader (which is seldom)	WRONG: If **you're** lost in the library . . . RIGHT: When **one** is lost in When **one** is lost in the library . . . .
altogether all	entirely	It's **altogether** too soon.
together	all in the same place	We're **all together** now.
break	to fracture, shatter, or ruin	Don't **break** my heart.
brake	a stopping device	Set the parking **brake**.

Table 8. A Guide for Evaluating Literature

Literary Character-istic	Basis for Judgement	Description/Evaluation	Remarks
Clarity of style	Works by Ernest Hemingway	Simple language, vivid description	Classic style
	Works by John Steinbeck	Clear language, depiction of real life experiences, believable and real characters	Often depressing themes
	Works by Ayn Rand	Logical thought, uses compari-sons of people as they are to people as they should be.	Idealistic and often pollyanna endings
	Works by Fyodor Dostoevsky	Well-defined, true-to-life characters, straight-line type develop-ment of characters	Characters almost become stereotyped.
Lack of Clarity	Works by James Joyce	Stream of consciousness style of writing, uses flashbacks, flash-forwards, element of unreality	Story line is often bewilder-ing and hard to follow. Relationships between events difficult to determine.
	Works by Edward Albee	Uses symbolism dealing with author's inner-most feelings, as typified by the play, **Tiny Alice.**	Difficult to understand, hard to relate to author's experi-ences because of symbolic plot structure.
Realism	Works by Fyodor Dostoevsky	Complicated plots dealing with real people true-to-life situations, and believable events, as typified by the novel **Crime and Punishment.**	

Literary Character-istic	Basis for Judgement	Description/ Evaluation	Remarks
Surrealism	Works by Anthony Burgess	Use of extremes and shock to develop satirical themes, as typified by the novel, **A Clockwork Orange.**	Language is virtually a foreign language. Must understand author's purpose in order to understand plot and theme.
Escapism	Works by Ian Fleming	Use of mystery and suspense. Themes tend to avoid serious life problems. Characters are heroic, larger than in life.	Typified by James Bond stories
	Works by J.R. Tolkien	Use of fantasy, Reality is suspended.	Fables—almost an Alice in Wonderland quality.
Theme of morality	Contrast **War and Peace** by Tolstoy with **Barabas** by Lagkervist	Moral conflicts. Hero is faced with a decision of what is morally right.	Often depressing yet important conflicts
Political Themes	Contrast **The Memoirs of Richard Nixon** with books written by John Dean, H.L. Halde-man, and John Erlichman	Political writings	Note how different authors treat the same historical event.
Religious	Contrast **Angels** by Billy Graham with **The Faith of a Rationalist** by Bertrand Russell	Theological writings. Develop extensive back-ground in both Eastern and Western theology.	Watch how each builds his case for or against theology.

Table 8. A Guide for Evaluating Literature *(continued)*

Literary Character- istic	Basis for Judgement	Description/ Evaluation	Remarks
Themes of philosophy	Contrast **The Communist Manifesto** by Karl Marx with **Atlas Shrugged** by Ayn Rand	Contrast extremes	Books with philosophical themes reflect opposites in the author's ideology
Artistic Detail	Works by Tennessee Williams	Economy of words ap- proaches poetry. Creation of character is based on creating empathy, as typified in the character of Blanche in the play **A Streetcar Named Desire**	Note usage of language, color and symbolism
	Works by Thomas Wolfe	Use of nostalgic des- cription, as typified by **Look Home- ward Angel.**	

Table 9. Organization of a Research Paper

PARTS	POINTS TO COVER
Introduction	Statement of Thesis Method of Gaining Reader's Interest and Attention Definition of Topic
Background	Historical Background of Topic Philosophical Background of Topic Significance of Topic Today
Arguments	Presentation of Contentions Facts Data Impact
Counter-Arguments	Presentation of Other Viewpoints Discussion of Other's Weaknesses Rebuttal
Summary	Conclusions Review of Best Argument Restatement of Thesis to Persuade End on Upbeat

Table 10. Eight Steps to Researching and Writing a Paper

STEP	DESCRIPTION
Gather Sources	Use most recently published material Locate five to twenty sources for most papers. Narrow your topic; limit the scope of the subject.
Compile Bibliography	List title, author, publisher, date and place of publication, volume and page numbers for all sources Number each source for reference in notes.
Preview and Evaluate	Browse through the material, beginning with easiest. Determine the most important information. Note location of information.
Prepare Notes	Prepare five pages, titled for each section of research paper.
Read	Only read information previously noted as important. Begin with easiest sources. Fill in note pages.
Check Notes	Look for gaps and fill. Review sources for additional data if necessary. Put in order.
Write	Use notes to structure paper logically. Use dictionary and thesaurus. Use powerful sentences and colorful examples. Type paper.
Proofread	Check for errors in logic, data, style, spelling and typing. Reread again at later time for fresh perspective. Polish and rewrite if required.